To Grandpa and
(Im on the fir

Love,
Esther x x x x

Poems From
Devon & Cornwall
Edited by Allison Jones

 Young**Writers**

First published in Great Britain in 2008 by:
Young Writers
Remus House
Coltsfoot Drive
Peterborough
PE2 9JX
Telephone: 01733 890066
Website: www.youngwriters.co.uk

SB ISBN 978-1 84431 452 2

Foreword

Young Writers was established in 1991 and has been passionately devoted to the promotion of reading and writing in children and young adults ever since. The quest continues today. Young Writers remains as committed to the nurturing of poetic and literary talent as ever.

This year's Young Writers competition has proven as vibrant and dynamic as ever and we are delighted to present a showcase of the best poetry from across the UK and in some cases overseas. Each poem has been selected from a wealth of *Little Laureates* entries before ultimately being published in this, our sixteenth primary school poetry series.

Once again, we have been supremely impressed by the overall quality of the entries we have received. The imagination, energy and creativity which has gone into each young writer's entry made choosing the poems a challenging and often difficult but ultimately hugely rewarding task - the general high standard of the work submitted ensured this opportunity to bring their poetry to a larger appreciative audience.

We sincerely hope you are pleased with this final collection and that you will enjoy *Little Laureates Poems From Devon & Cornwall* for many years to come.

Contents

Ben Tunnicliffe (10)	26
Samuel Wills (10)	26
Amelia Hickey (10)	26
Kathryn Anne Butcher (10)	27
Reese Fox (10)	27
Gabby Amy Dey (11)	27
James Stocker (10)	28

Exeter Road Primary School, Exmouth
Deanna Vernon (10)	28

Gorran Primary School, St Austell
Rosa Dyer (10)	29
Isabel Semple (9)	29
Hayden Standing (9)	30
Naomi Pascoe (9)	30
Harvey Howson (10)	30
Jennifer Dowling (10)	31
Jacob Fletcher (9)	32
Liam Gouldsmith (9)	32
Lucy Barkhuysen (9)	33
Chloe West (9)	33
Selina Wheeley (9)	34
Billy Meneer (9)	34

Gwinear Community Primary School, Hayle
Anna Horigan (10)	35
Ben Skuse (10)	35
Reave Kendall (10)	36
Dalian Paul (9)	37

Jacobstow Community Primary School, Bude
Charlotte Booker (7)	38
Jack Biggs (7)	38
Sabrina Harris (8)	39
Frank Barriball (8)	39
Christopher Turner (7)	40
Molly Nutt (8)	40
Jodie Bowman (8)	41
Chloe Tilley (8)	41

Renée Barry (10)	60
Charlotte Benwell (10)	60
Danielle Green (10)	61
Lucas Woodbridge (11)	61
Hannah Humphries (10)	62
Amber Stearman (10)	62
Heidi Steer (10)	63
Danielle English (11)	63
Kana Tachibana-Doyle (10)	64
Jenny Cox (11)	64
Katie Cook (10)	64
Jacob Warner (11)	65
Jasmine Hancock (10)	65
Ryan Finn (11)	65
Curtis Hallett (11)	66
Samantha Townsend (10)	66
Aimée Ruffle (10)	67
Bryony Butler (10)	67

Marlborough Primary School, Falmouth

Elissia Roberts (10)	68
Olivia Morrison (10)	68

Mount Charles Primary School, St Austell

Isabel Stephens (10)	69
Rosie Mingo (7)	69
Laura Holman (10)	70
Charlie Retallick (9)	70
Thea Rowley (9)	71
Jessica Trahair (9)	71
Daniel Watkins (7)	72
Amber Dumbleton (10)	72
Jayd Cloughton-Kehoe (10)	73
Bryher Semonin (7)	73
Carla Aldington (9)	74
Sophie Weedon (11)	74
Florence Strookman (7)	75
Katie Wenmouth (7)	75
Danni Rickard (10)	75
April Talbot (7)	76

Georgia Rawling (9)	76
Summer Williams (9)	77
Rachel Pinder (7)	77
Teri Trevains (8)	78
Bernice Barnes (10)	78
Milo Semonin (9)	78
Rositta Caesar (10)	79
Noah Semonin (10)	79

Mount Street Primary School, Plymouth

Shanice Morrison (8)	80
Lucas Booker-Munoz (8)	80
Natalia Hempsall (8)	81
Joseph Tiernan (9)	81
Kamila Amer (9)	82
Lauren Kerry (8)	82
Katie Brown (9)	82
Heaven Fenn (8)	83
Isabel Davies (8)	83
Corey Blackmore (10)	83
Emily McArthur (10)	84
Brandon Joll (9)	84
Travis Haydon (10)	85
Conner Mitchell (11)	85
Cameron Moule (9)	86
Michael Pascoe (8)	86
Fahad (8)	87
Bethany Pennington (8)	87
Alisha Pennington (10)	88
Connor Mitchell (10)	88
Tanaka Mudimu Jimalo (10)	88
Florence Sullivan (9)	88
Isaac Davies (9)	89
Richard Sharman (11)	89
Kyah Brooks (9)	89
Jake Rout (10)	89
Katie Smyth (8)	90
Liga Ozolina (9)	90
Tino Mwadeyi (10)	91
Elisabeth Temlett-Dixon (10)	91

Jacob Foran (10)   91
Bailey White (9)   92

Newton Ferrers CE Primary School, Plymouth
Tanya Pearson & Molly Finch (9)   92
Joshua Eason (9) & Phoebe Rhead (10)   93
Joshua Turner (8) & Jeremy Eason (9)   93
Erik Wilson (9), Aimee Burlinson & James Wall (10)   94
Fergus Carruthers (9) & Freddy Hillier (10)   94
Ben Harvey (8) & Ben King (10)   95
Imogen Tarran (9)   95
Nathan King (8) & Juliet Hepburn (9)   96
Max Lawes (8) & James Willis (10)   96
Georgina McCartney (8), Tom Mears (9)
                               & Bryony Lawes (10)   97

Pondhu Primary School, St Austell
Samantha England (10)   97
Anthony Sanders (11)   98
Sam Loud (10)   98
Hannah Orchard (10)   98
Amy Littler (10)   99
Daisy Carr (11)   99
Cavan Boyer (11)   99
Breon Wickett (10)   100
Laura McDonald (10)   100
Bridie Gabriel (10)   101
Samuel Rowley (10)   101
Jamie Sanders (11)   101
Hayden Thompson (10)   102
William Musgrave (10)   102
Chad Busby (11)   102
Keyna Summers (11)   103
Nicole Gilbert (10)   103
Thomas Tyrrell (10)   103
Shannon Caulfield (10)   104
Hannah Noy (11)   104
Chad Ackrell (10)   104
Jade Truman (10)   105

St Buryan Primary School, Penzance

Emma Rowe (9)	105
Olivia Barnes (9)	105
Ana Young (9)	106
Luke Piggott (10)	106
Justine Nixon (10)	106
Kellie Williams (9)	107
Tegen Butterfield (10)	107
Jakob Fox (10)	108
Laura Sutton (10)	108
Abbey Thomas (9)	109
Shannon Harris (10)	109
Imogen Forster (9)	110
James Margerison (10)	111
Haydn Tremethick (10)	111
Charlotte Trembath (9)	111
Caitlin Eley (10)	112
Teigan Delbridge (9)	112
Tom Price (9)	112
Cameron Ness (10)	113
Jacob Cowell (9)	113
Bethany Mason (10)	113
Ross Thomas (10)	114

St Day & Caharrack Community School, Redruth

Patryk Rudnik (11) & Oliver Cornell (10)	114
Holly Summerson (10)	115
Holly Truman (10)	115
Ella Jarvis (10)	116
Katie Jones (11)	116
Tamara Orchard (10)	117
Chloe Roberts (10)	117
Isabella Cochrane (10)	118
Joe Goldsworthy (9)	118
Katie Fletcher (9)	119
Chloe Dingle (10)	119
Jasmine Bennetts (9)	119

St John's RC Primary School, Tiverton

Charlotte Rogers (10)	120
Jordan Haskings (10)	121

Yealmpstone Farm Primary School

The Poems

The Buzzard

Viewing, searching, staring,
Scanning the fruitful earth.

Swooping, gliding, spying,
Hovering menacingly above its prey.

Plummeting, pursuing, plunging,
Clinging on to the unfortunate quarry.

Pouncing, gripping, penetrating,
Pinning the prey to the ground.

Malicious, vicious, pitiless,
Ruthlessly ripping the defeated victim.

Magnificent, majestic, silken birds,
Hunting to survive.

Esther Beyer (9)
Blackpool CE Primary School, Liverton

Falling In Love

Falling in love is pink,
Like a soft fluffy teddy.

It smells like perfume,
Sweet and fragrant.

It tastes like lips,
When you have your first kiss.

It feels like a roller coaster,
When your tummy turns inside out.

It looks like pink love hearts,
Floating in the air.

It reminds me of summer,
When the sun is shining brightly.

Kylah Leworthy (10)
Bratton Fleming Community Primary School, Barnstaple

Melancholy

Melancholy is shadowy
like a bear loitering in a cave.
It tastes like sharp sour grapes.
It feels like a bristly dull bramble bush.
It looks like a volcanic rock in a volvic crater.
It sounds like an explosion from a jet plane
colliding with the Earth.
It reminds me of a black widow spider
injecting venom into its prey.

Samuel James Hawkins (10)
Bratton Fleming Community Primary School, Barnstaple

Joy

Joy is yellow like the bright glowing sun
on a hot summer's day.
It looks like a rainbow, shimmering in the rain.
It feels like waking up on Christmas Day,
snowflakes drifting out of the sky.
It tastes like fresh strawberries
dipped in sweet, thick chocolate sauce.

Kerry Ellen Parkin (10)
Bratton Fleming Community Primary School, Barnstaple

Darkness

It is black like the night sky.
It sounds like raging gunfire.
It looks like ghostly shadows at midnight.
It tastes like venomous berries.
It reminds me of whistling arrows and clashing swords.
It feels like a chilly, gloomy mist on a winter's eve.

Jack Hewlett (10)
Bratton Fleming Community Primary School, Barnstaple

Rage

It's black like a farmer who's lost all his sheep.
It looks like a broken bike.
It sounds like someone being eaten alive.
It reminds me of a scorpion's sting.
It smells like rotting horse dung.
It tastes like overcooked, rotten carrots.

Eric Thomas Ridd (9)
Bratton Fleming Community Primary School, Barnstaple

Laughter

It looks like words in the air
It reminds me of a poem that people giggle at
It tastes like happiness
It sounds like movement
Its colour is yellow
It feels like a word
It smells like round yellow sweets.

Joe Bond (9)
Bratton Fleming Community Primary School, Barnstaple

Rage

Rage is red, an angry red.
It looks like a frosty day.
It tastes like a sour lemon.
It smells like gone-off egg.
It reminds me of beeping horns in traffic jams.
It sounds like infuriating rhinos.
It feels like waking up on Mondays.

Rowanne Smith (9)
Bratton Fleming Community Primary School, Barnstaple

Darkness

Darkness is dark black like a midnight panther
It sounds like the mutterings of a mad old man
It tastes like a troll's black heart
It looks like an evil parasite that eats you from inside
It feels like oozing scab pus
It smells like rotten flesh
It reminds me of things that attack you in your nightmares.

Conor Bellis (10)
Bratton Fleming Community Primary School, Barnstaple

Hunger

Hunger is black like tyres, big and bold.
Hunger feels painful like falling over when you're old.
It reminds me of a dark night when everyone is asleep.
It smells like gone-off cheese left on the side.
It tastes like sour lemons that never fill you up.

Laura Shapland (9)
Bratton Fleming Community Primary School, Barnstaple

Horror

Horror is black
It smells like rotten bananas
It sounds like rumbling thunder
It tastes like Stilton cheese
It feels like dripping blood
It reminds me of fear.

Chris Dennis (9)
Bratton Fleming Community Primary School, Barnstaple

Fun

Fun's colours are bright yellow and pink,
It sounds like disco music,
It reminds me of tap dancing,
It smells like freshly cooked hot dogs,
It looks like brightly coloured balloons and fairy cakes on a plate,
It feels like excitement running down my spine,
It tastes like yummy crisps being crunched.

Emma Huxtable (9)
Bratton Fleming Community Primary School, Barnstaple

Hunger

Hunger is brown like an asteroid colliding into the moon.
It tastes like a rotten sour lemon on a dark cloudy day.
It looks like a scrawny elephant on its last legs.
It sounds like a deafening siren that never stops.
It reminds me of a painfully sharp needle jabbing into your skin.

Jonah Langston (10)
Bratton Fleming Community Primary School, Barnstaple

Silence

Silence, it's like an empty forgotten tomb.
It feels like dry sand running through your toes.
It tastes like flat lemonade - no bubbles.
It smells like sweet lemon cake.
It's white, like a blank sheet of paper.

Chester Clay (9)
Bratton Fleming Community Primary School, Barnstaple

Joy

Joy is yellow like the sun's shooting rays.
It tastes like a triple chocolate cake.
It sounds like Mum calling, 'Dinner's ready!'
It reminds me of opening a present on Christmas Day.
It feels like the handlebars of a bike.

Kai Chapple (9)
Bratton Fleming Community Primary School, Barnstaple

Melancholy

Melancholy is light grey like a thick mist and dark clouds
                                                    dripping with rain.
It's like thick dust after a long holiday.
It's like wind howling in a valley.
It's like soggy semolina gone mouldy.
It reminds me of very deep water in the middle of the ocean.

Tom Dunbavin (9)
Bratton Fleming Community Primary School, Barnstaple

Envy

Envy is dark green
It feels like a crumbling cookie
It sounds like Christmas baubles crashing
It tastes of mouldy carrots
It looks like a broken light
It smells like soggy mud
It reminds me of a rabbit when it's ill.

Reuben Langston (8)
Bratton Fleming Community Primary School, Barnstaple

Young Writers - Little Laureates Poems From Devon & Cornwall

Horror

It reminds me of death clawing at my throat.
It sounds like a wolf howling at a full moon.
It smells like rotten autumn apples in an orchard.
It tastes like sherbet lemons cutting through my tongue.
It feels like a child lost in a maze.

Ashley Wright (10)
Bratton Fleming Community Primary School, Barnstaple

Envy

It sounds like a thundercloud echoing through the sky.
It feels like a rotten blueberry gone to waste.
It tastes like sour milk curdling in the kitchen cupboard.
It looks like a forgotten tree whistling for help.

Jack Heal (9)
Bratton Fleming Community Primary School, Barnstaple

Fun

Fun is blue like the crisp morning sky.
It feels like glossy wrapping paper when you open a present.
It sounds like the bang of party poppers going off
and the confetti spraying out.
It tastes like tomatoey, cheesy, saucy pasta.
It looks like a gingerbread house made of sweets
and dripping chocolate.

Alex Mullen (10)
Bratton Fleming Community Primary School, Barnstaple

Darkness

Darkness is black,
Like a rabbit's burrow.

It feels like you have some chocolate,
But someone takes it away.

It sounds like there's no one around to talk to,
Like a teddy that's been dropped on the street.

It tastes like soggy Brussels sprouts,
All mushed up in a dish.

It looks like someone who's lost,
On their own with no one to help.

It reminds me of flowers,
That have no sun to enjoy a new day.

Amie Balman (9)
Bratton Fleming Community Primary School, Barnstaple

Silence

Silence is white, boring and blank.
It reminds me of an empty classroom waiting for dawn.
It smells like water.
It tastes like plain pasta.
It sounds like the emptiness on a wild moor.

Shelby Gregory (10)
Bratton Fleming Community Primary School, Barnstaple

Horror

Horror, it is pitch-black like pouncing tarantulas.
It sounds like little feet going *pitter-patter, pitter-patter.*
It looks like a furry fuzz ball ready to jump.
It feels like a hairy creature crawling all over my hand.
It reminds me of being in Terror World Amusement Park.

Jonathan Bowden (9)
Bratton Fleming Community Primary School, Barnstaple

Melancholy

Melancholy is grey like clouds invading the blue sky.
It feels like the smoothest pebbles on the beaches of the world
being jaggered down by sandpaper.
It smells like the gorgeous smell of petrol being taken away
by the car doors.
It tastes like the juiciest fruits on the planets being shrivelled up
by a draught.
It reminds me of the scorching hot days on the beach but no surf!

Rhys Morrison (10)
Bratton Fleming Community Primary School, Barnstaple

Rage

It feels like being powerless when threatened by danger.
It tastes like bones grating across your teeth.
It sounds like a lion's deep rumbling growls before it pounces.
It looks like the eyes of a haunted bloodshot man.
It reminds me of when a tsunami wave engulfs the land!

Max Tunnicliffe (9)
Bratton Fleming Community Primary School, Barnstaple

Black Cats And Pointed Hats

Today in the park I saw a witch
She had a wart on her nose
A pointed hat on her head
That sight gave me funny dreams when I went to bed
Today in the woods I saw a witch
She had a long nose with a wart on the end
I didn't point it out because I didn't like to offend
I'm telling you, too, so you can share my delight
Of watching witches, black cats and pointed hats.

Ellie Davies (10)
Brixton St Mary's CE Primary School, Brixton

Sunshine

S un shimmering in the sky,
U mbrellas popping up for shade,
N ightfall, sun disappears,
S un, hot as ever,
H appy again in the sun,
I n the shade you're wasting your time,
N ever enough sun,
E ntering the sun makes it fun.

Leyte Prouse (10)
Brixton St Mary's CE Primary School, Brixton

Football

F ootball is a great sport,
O ther people have teams they support,
O n the pitch they are keen,
T hey have eleven people on each team,
B ut managers are strict,
A fter one person is kicked
L osing is bad.
L ike me they go mad.

Millie Springbett (9)
Brixton St Mary's CE Primary School, Brixton

Pirates

I sail the seas
To attack and loot
With a patch on my eye
And a wooden leg
A cutlass by my side and a brace of pistols
With biscuits and rum for tea
So why don't you come
To rob and loot with me?

Liam Johns (10)
Brixton St Mary's CE Primary School, Brixton

The Day

It could be sunny
It could be rainy
But you know it's never the same
It could be thundering
It could be dull
But you know it's never the same
It could be windy
It could be lightning
But you know it's never the same
There could be dogs
There could be cats
There could be anything
There could be a bird
There could be anything!

Vicky Tarrant (9)
Brixton St Mary's CE Primary School, Brixton

Ocean

Ocean waves sway left to right
All through the winter night
Crabs snap
Ducks quack
And dolphins are leaping
When everyone is sleeping
With a big splash
They go to bed as quick as a flash
But fish stay awake
In the lake
When the sun arrives
Frogs go to catch flies
The fish are feeling nappy
While all the others are happy.

Courtney Osborne (9)
Brixton St Mary's CE Primary School, Brixton

Friends At School

When you start school,
You don't have many friends,
Then one day you play with someone,
Your first friend ever,
Over time you make more,
More friends,
The last few days you argue, you fall out,
The next day, when they think the time is right,
They come to apologise,
Over time this will happen,
Happen to friends at school.

Sean Chislett (9)
Brixton St Mary's CE Primary School, Brixton

Football

F ootball is a very good sport
O ther teams score goals
O ften players go to other countries
T ackle defenders away
B alls go thundering past the goalkeeper
A ny team can play well
L eap up when players score
L aughing at players when they get a red card!

Alex Godwin (9)
Brixton St Mary's CE Primary School, Brixton

Elephant

Down in the jungle
Where nobody goes
There's a very large elephant
Swinging his trunk, having some fun
He goes and makes a dam
Elephants are cool
Elephants are fat
Elephants are stupid
And that is how we do the rap!

Rosie Elms (9)
Brixton St Mary's CE Primary School, Brixton

Dinosaurs

D angerous creatures
I n prehistoric times.
N ext there is Triassic.
O mnivores, predators, plant-eaters.
S ome may eat you.
A whole new species.
U h-oh, you better watch out!
R emember we're not alone.
S o look out, here they come!

Reece Slemon (9)
Brixton St Mary's CE Primary School, Brixton

Sun

Sun burning bright as light,
Shimmering, sparkling and no wind in sight,
A cloud creeping over the sun
With the gleaming power . . .
It rushes away with a sunburn
As it goes through the years,
I will always be there as I stare
Through the dark days and the light.

Celeste Pierre (9)
Brixton St Mary's CE Primary School, Brixton

Stranded

Abandoned by Mother
Dragged out to sea
Sinking, sinking, down, down
Crawling backwards at the bottom of the sea
Sticky sand just like glue
Legs are stuck, stuck, stuck
Pulling, pulling
Then rip! My leg is torn from my body
Like paper from a pad!

Ashley Cotter (9)
Castle Primary School, Tiverton

A Cool Day Out At Croyde

I see a shell that looks like snakeskin.
I see big rocks that look like icebergs.
I see sticks that look like bones.
I see Lundy Island in the distance that looks like a
                                    lump of steak floating.
I feel that there is ocean in me.

Danny Crook (9)
Castle Primary School, Tiverton

Seaside Senses

I can see the sea glistening like blue crystals,
I can feel the wind rushing through my hair,
I can hear the roaring sea like a hungry lion,
I can taste my sweet ice cream melting in my mouth,

I can see spiky rocks that look like old castles,
I can feel the sun beating down on my face,
I can feel the soft sand brushing in-between my toes,
I can hear the sea rushing against the shore,
I can taste the salt from the sea in the air.

Ruth Maddicks (9)
Castle Primary School, Tiverton

What I See

A limpet shell looks like a fluorescent stained-glass window,
The rocks look like mini mountains of danger,
I see a floating flute washed into the sea,
I see clouds of fluffy rice coming out of a cooker,
I see little people inside me moving me and making me think.

Honour James (9)
Castle Primary School, Tiverton

A Day In Imagination

The sea is like a giant lake
The cloud is like a dragon flying gently through the sky
A hornet hovers across the grass
There's a smell that can drift you away
Three crabs crawling back to the sea
Under the water they drift away
In the end they may finish up in America!

Joseph Mulligan (9)
Castle Primary School, Tiverton

The Raggedy Sea

The sea is like a screwed up piece of blue tissue,
There's a nice, metallic, shiny, orange pebble reflecting in the sun,
There are huge, pointy, jagged rocks like mountains bursting
out of the sand,
Behind the horizon there are huge pirate ships with infamous
bloodthirsty pirates drinking rum.

Robert Kingdon (10)
Castle Primary School, Tiverton

Seaside

In an ordinary country, there's an ordinary sea.
In the ordinary sea, there's a land waiting for me.
I see dimly in the distance, I cannot see a thing
Except for volcanoes,
I can just see volcanoes exploding and erupting
Until land pulls out of the sea.

Chloë-Rose Jones (9)
Castle Primary School, Tiverton

Sea Senses At Croyde

I can see a jagged, purple, stripy shell, with a white hole.
In the middle distance, I see lots of volcanoes and lava
which are rocks and water.
Behind the sea, I can see a beautiful new world
where lots of flowers grow and horses gallop.
This is a place where everyone is kind and no one ever fights.

Lois Mackerness (9)
Castle Primary School, Tiverton

The Sea

The sea is like a shining blue sun,
A shimmering carpet of blue,
A roaring train,
The whistling of the thin wind,
My nose grasps the scent of the salt in the air,
The wind is light,
The sun is exposing its warmth,
I adore the sun,
It's warm and calm,
I can hear the waves edging nearer and nearer,
Dead lonely crabs,
Their faces still gloomy with dark envy,
The sand is ingrained with rock,
A pale orange speckle,
I'm a rock
That has floated across the dangerous sea
After my life has abandoned me,
I am lost, cold and lonely,
I have been eroded,
My life is slipping away,
I soon know it is my last day,

Now I am soft, disappearing sand!

Tashan Best (10)
Castle Primary School, Tiverton

It's Like . . .

The fierce blue sea is like a crumpled bed
The breathing sun is like a roaring heater
The ozone air is like salt on my chips
The sand on my feet is like me in my slippers

The sand-coloured shells are like the colours on the cliffs
The cracks in the rocks are like the wrinkles on an old person.

William Newcombe (9)
Castle Primary School, Tiverton

Alone On The Beach

I'm on the beach
All alone
Can't see anything
All I can smell
Is miserable wind
Blowing in my face
A picture in my head tells me
Something is coming
It is a boy
Now I'm safe!

Ashley Pike (9)
Castle Primary School, Tiverton

A Lion Roaring

The sea is like a giant blue bathtub
I can hear the cars like a lion roaring to the sea
I can hear traffic like a tornado coming closer
I can smell the fresh grass that's just been cut.

Toby Park (9)
Castle Primary School, Tiverton

A Day At The Sea

I am near the sea
I am shiny
I am a pebble.
I am trapped in a forest which is dark, cold and spooky.
I can see an island like a lot of flats.
Beyond the horizon there is purple and green monster waiting to play.
I see a horse trying to eat me!

Fiona Pike (10)
Castle Primary School, Tiverton

Pebbles Of Mountains

There's a land of pebbles that look like mountains.

I see pointed rocks going into the air with the rough sea crashing behind them.

I see an island, it looks like a massive turtle swimming.

Beyond my sight there is a dark island with violent monsters trapped behind a massive wall.

I feel inside me, Vikings having a massive party, eating and drinking.

Lewis White (10)
Castle Primary School, Tiverton

The Beautiful Coast

The coasts are warm and cosy with the sun beaming
on all the people sunbathing, being relaxed.
The children in the sea having the best time of their lives,
and dogs running everywhere being wild.

Keeley Seatherton (9)
Castle Primary School, Tiverton

What Can I See?

I can see all different amazing colours of shells
I see rocks which make me feel like I'm in a rocky jungle
I can just see an island, like it wants to be invisible
Beyond the island I think I can see a volcano in the sea
loudly erupting
I can see myself on the island looking at the volcano.

Samantha Taplin (9)
Castle Primary School, Tiverton

A Great Day At Croyde

A lawnmower sounds like a bumblebee.
The sea smells like a swimming pool.
It makes me nice and cosy on the beach.
A crab shell looks really rough on the outside.
The sea is really rough.

Brandon Vellacott (10)
Castle Primary School, Tiverton

A Great Day At Croyde

Rocks, rocks everywhere, gathering round.
Sparkling everywhere, every day all different shapes.
I see tall mountains with little people at the top.
I see a floating pencil, a forest all over.
I see puffs coming to carry me away and taste the fresh blue sea.

Kieran Tebby (9)
Castle Primary School, Tiverton

Croyde Sea Senses

I can see a shiny upside-down shell,
In the middle distance I can see spiky icebergs,
On the horizon I can see an enormous rock called Lundy,
Beyond the horizon I can see a beautiful land of rainbows
                                    and nice kind kids,
My heart is beating with excitement to go beyond the horizon!

Sophie West (9)
Castle Primary School, Tiverton

Island

I can see an island that looks like a stretched-out boat
With a glamorous spark on the tip of the island.
I can smell the salt in the roaring sea.
On the back of my neck is the strong breezy wind.
The sea sounds like an aeroplane flying over the land.

Lewis Brooks (10)
Castle Primary School, Tiverton

Beautiful Lily

Lily
Soft blossom wavers in the gentle breeze,
Pale amber stalk soaring high, like a soldier on alert,
Dewdrops like diamonds on a glamorous woman, wearing
a white dress,
With a blemish, it cuts through the horizon line, slender and sleek,
Bottle-green leaves supporting the marvellous trumpet of pollen,
Lily,
Beautiful lily!

Jake Crossland (11)
Chudleigh Knighton CE Primary School, Newton Abbot

Sailing

As you zoom along, the sea breeze gently tickles your face
There are lots of people shouting, 'Port!' and 'Starboard!'
The waves look like bubble wrap on the boat.
The sails are like wings carrying you on the water
And you float on the water like a dainty little leaf bobbing on the surf.

Jemima Crossland (10)
Chudleigh Knighton CE Primary School, Newton Abbot

Life On A Farm

The fearsome fox,
Hedgehog in box,
Fluffy chick's nest,
The hen knows best,
Happy horse neighs,
He likes to graze,
Life on a farm,
Field mouse and barn!

Sam James (9)
Crowan Primary School, Camborne

Rugby World Cup

The competition was held in France,
And some of the teams did a funny dance,
England fought their way through,
But South Africa did too,
With Wilkinson's boot,
He had a good shoot,
We nearly had a try,
But we did not cry.

Jonathan Vincet (9)
Crowan Primary School, Camborne

Football Crazy

The football team is on the pitch,
They strike the ball without a hitch,
One of the players is not very tall,
He attacks and tackles and passes the ball,
The crowd cheers as a goal is scored,
Darth Vader comes out with his lightsaber sword,
He runs down the pitch chasing them quick,
The crowd goes wild as he scores a hat-trick.

Harry Hawken (10)
Crowan Primary School, Camborne

Monkey World

Chimps in the enclosure over there
Sitting in the corner, the cheeky pair
Walking around I see the baboons
Watching the children with their balloons
Turning round I see the apes
Playing and eating bananas and grapes
Ten minutes later I meet the gorillas
Munching on lettuce and spicy tortillas.

Luke Ellis (10)
Crowan Primary School, Camborne

The City

Bustling people drifting by,
All look up to the clear blue sky,
An amazing aeroplane overhead,
Zooming into a cloudy bed,
Small, big, tall and short,
Each building of a different sort,
Vegetables, fruit, clothes and toys,
But most of the toys are for boys.

Sam Johns (10)
Crowan Primary School, Camborne

The Countryside

The countryside is green and brown,
With lots of things growing in the ground.
The farmer has a lot of veg,
Like carrots, potatoes and cabbage.
The horses and cattle graze in the fields,
While the farmer is busy bringing in the yield.
Pigs, cows and chickens are everywhere,
To roam the land that we all share.

Sennen Mustafa (10)
Crowan Primary School, Camborne

My Friend Bobby Duck

I have a friend called Bobby Duck,
Who's always getting very stuck.
I threw a ball whilst sat in bed,
It came back down and hit his head.
He said he wanted to be a cat,
I gave him string - he tangled that.
And so I said to my friend Bobby,
'Have you got a proper hobby?'
He led me through the pitch-black dark,
All the way into the park.
We found the pond and he jumped in,
He said his hobby was to swim!

Celia King (10)
Crowan Primary School, Camborne

No Nothing!

No children
No parks
No light
No dark
No hair
No head
No children
No bed
No birds that sing
No bells that ring

No nothing!

Nicole Wilson (10)
Crowan Primary School, Camborne

The Plug Hole Monster

Watch your finger!
Do not linger!
Water whooshing
He is pushing
Wants his meal
Don't you squeal?
Bathtub baddy
Who's the daddy?

Ben James (9)
Crowan Primary School, Camborne

Hallowe'en Hotpot

Blackhead of greasy skin,
In the cauldron simmering,
Hair of nose and wax of ear,
Scurf of scalp and salt of tear,
Sticky eye and fur of tongue,
Plaque of tooth and blood of gum.
For a spell at the double,
Bring it to the boil
          And bubble!

Danielle Richards (10)
Crowan Primary School, Camborne

Rock Pools

Sharper than razors, smoother than silk,
Rock pools filled with seawater and silt.
Deep beneath hides a secret marine,
Filled with sea life that fights to the extreme.
Slimy, slippery, squelchy seaweed,
Swirling, whirling, around my feet.
Cockles, mussels, pebbles and sea,
This is a treat for a beachcomber like me!

Jessica Buckler (10)
Crowan Primary School, Camborne

Supercar

Lamborghini, big and fast,
A supercar built to last,
The coolest, crafted car you'll see,
All my mates so jealous of me.

Nought to sixty in just a second,
The craziest car on Earth I reckon,
A perfect performance every time,
I'm so lucky, it's all mine!

Ben Tunnicliffe (10)
Crowan Primary School, Camborne

A Sweetheart

You will always be my sweetheart,
We will never be apart,
It was on that romantic night,
That you became my knight,
That day you asked me to marry you,
I said those famous words, 'I do!'
We will be together from now to death,
All the way to my final breath.

Samuel Wills (10)
Crowan Primary School, Camborne

Fairies

Fairies fluttering by the sea
They are all staring at me
I have never seen them run
In the lovely midday sun
Flying around like a bird in the sky
I watch the fairies flutter by
Every day I go back home to sleep
In a flash they're all in the deep.

Amelia Hickey (10)
Crowan Primary School, Camborne

Lollipops

Orange, yellow, green and red
All these colours in your head
Sucking softly on your lollipop
That you bought today at the sweet shop
Lollipops, they are the best
So much better than the rest
Orange, lemon, lime and cherry
All these flavours make you merry.

Kathryn Anne Butcher (10)
Crowan Primary School, Camborne

Football Crazy

I'm football crazy,
I'm not at all lazy,
I'm football mad,
I'm not at all bad,
I like to keep fit,
No one gets a hit,
In the league match,
Goals get snatched!

Reese Fox (10)
Crowan Primary School, Camborne

Through The Window

From the window I can see
All the cows looking at me.
Trucking and spluttering goes the engine,
People on the train laughing and cluttering.
There are some children skipping and joking,
All of the adults talking and smoking.
Then I see some flashy lights,
All of them giving me such a fright!

Gabby Amy Dey (11)
Crowan Primary School, Camborne

Hallowe'en Fright

Witches and goblins soar through the night,
Swooping and swerving, what a terrible fright.
Pumpkins stare from window ledges,
And skeletons hide in prickly hedges.
Beware the trick or treaters roam,
Along the street to visit your home.
Sniggering, shouting, spooky, scary,
But one little girl has dressed as a fairy.
When the doorbell rings or you hear a knock,
Open the door and wait for a shock!

James Stocker (10)
Crowan Primary School, Camborne

Anderson Shelter

A girl cramped and squashed.
N o food to eat, except in dreams.
D inner will not be eaten.
E ver and ever bombs will never stop,
R oofs of sheds will be blown off.
S ounds will always be mumbled.
O n and on you can hear people's screams.
N oises are like swarms of bees travelling through the air.

S helves have been sent flying through the air.
H ouses have been torn to bits.
E ndless deaths for people everywhere.
L ives are lost without shelters.
T ea will soon come.
E veryone's food will come.
R aid is over, time to eat!

Deanna Vernon (10)
Exeter Road Primary School, Exmouth

Wind Spirit

Dancing and weaving his arms around rooted figures, his heart
long gone and dead,
Dragging his misty shadow behind as he searches for a flicker of joy,
His voice is the wind that rattles the windows of his betrothed
so old and weak,
Sadness and regret are his only feelings and the exhaustion of
a thousand years of restless thoughts,
He knows no one and no one knows he for he is forgotten in the living
world,
His tears are the dew that blankets the grass of an early
autumn morning,
Soulful and lonely is he,
For he and his battered mind are wistfully spirited away.

Rosa Dyer (10)
Gorran Primary School, St Austell

Fear

You could hear the rumble from the faraway land,
Its massive feet thumping through the soil,
The world turned even faster when it came,
Its gloomy eyes staring through the forest,
Drips of goo following it wherever it went,
Hairs growing from its fat belly,
A flock of seagulls flew over when it came,
The villagers were gone,
Suddenly . . .
Its massive feet squished all the houses,
The goo dripping from its body stuck the villagers together,
Its goofy teeth bent down to eat them,
Everyone had been waiting for this moment.

Isabel Semple (9)
Gorran Primary School, St Austell

Food

Doughnuts are round, sugary and sweet
This is a food that I like to eat.

Sprouts are green, stinky and horrible
It's a real shame because they look so adorable.

Sausages come from a pig
They are fat, juicy and big.

Strawberries are my favourite food
They always put me in a good mood.

Hayden Standing (9)
Gorran Primary School, St Austell

Love To Dance

I have always loved to dance
Ballet, modern and tap
I am lucky to have the chance
And I love it when people clap.

I feel as light as a feather
When I am dancing all day long
I dance whatever the weather
And I feel things can't go wrong.

Naomi Pascoe (9)
Gorran Primary School, St Austell

What Is It?

In the pale moonlight it howls.
Hiding in the darkness as it creeps around.
Sometimes it is spotted as it strides into a beam of moonlight,
And if you happen to meet it face to face, eye to eye,
It will gobble you up!

Harvey Howson (10)
Gorran Primary School, St Austell

Spirits

The spirits started to sing, their light voices touched me,
a wave spread over me, I heard a soft voice saying, 'Come, come.'
I wanted to go, I would, *No!*

The singing stopped, the spirits' voices no longer sounded soft
and beautiful, their hair no longer a beautiful sheaf of corn
but a ragged bunch of weeds waiting to be torn from its socket.
A glimpse of silk was the only beauty that could be bestowed
upon such poor creatures.
The spirits had ventured into a land unknown to them,
they had ventured into *anger!*

They were moving, pulling me with them,
I was trapped, my hands tore at the bubble surrounding me,
I couldn't get out!

They were taking me with them, their once beautifully carved faces
now clumps of rotten wood.
I could see their beastly faces monitoring my every movement,
I was trapped, I couldn't get out!

The evil spirits' bedraggled bodies were closing around me
once more, their once smiling expressions now a look of sorrow
and menace, then once again the agile voice spoke
but this time the words were different, it was whispering in a voice that
still stood strong and it was saying, 'It is time, it is time,'
and all at once I knew my fate!

The spirits hesitated and then drew back their grasp,
their bony hands leaving my shoulders in a swift movement,
it was time!

I was gliding, gliding across a silent lake, my jeans had disappeared,
in their place was a silken dress of the lightest fabric.
I felt for my legs but they were not there and then I knew it . . .
I had joined them.

Jennifer Dowling (10)
Gorran Primary School, St Austell

World War II

Soldiers marching,
Enemy laughing,
Concentration all around.
Children crying,
Soldiers dying,
Sadness all around.

Machine guns firing,
War is tiring,
Madness all around.
War is over,
Planes no longer
Coming over.
Calmness all around.

Jacob Fletcher (9)
Gorran Primary School, St Austell

My Cat Chloe

My cat is called Chloe
Not Tiger or Snowy
Her coat is black
From front to back
She likes to lie in the sun
And she also likes to have fun
Chloe likes to lie on my bed
On a blanket which is green and red.

Liam Gouldsmith (9)
Gorran Primary School, St Austell

The Sea

As the waves crash onto the harbour,
the seagulls screech in fright.
The cormorants dive to catch a fish,
as the white horses start to die.
The sun is peeking over the hill as people start to arrive,
and, as a net skims the water, the fish dart away.
As the sun starts to set, the people get ready to leave.
The gulls go back to their nests
and everything is quiet, except the sea.
The sea is still there, the sea is always there!

Lucy Barkhuysen (9)
Gorran Primary School, St Austell

My Dog Ollie

I have a dog called Ollie
he's a complete and utter wally.
When you carry him, he's fairly light
but when you blow a raspberry
he jumps up with fright.

When he sees a bubble
there's a big sign of trouble.
Ollie likes to chase his tail
he likes to eat a tasty snail!

Chloe West (9)
Gorran Primary School, St Austell

Do You Believe In Fairies?

Delicate fairies dancing
In the forest
Moonlight shining
On precious wings.

Flowery swirling dresses
Touch the dewy grass
They tiptoe around
Soft voices giggling.

Flapping wings from
Toadstool to toadstool
Chatting about teeth
Happy in their work.

Celebrating sparkling memories
Of happy children
Who have lost a tooth
And believe in fairies.

Selina Wheeley (9)
Gorran Primary School, St Austell

You And Me

I am sitting here on this tree writing this poem for you and me.
I can hear the buzzing of the bumblebees next to me,
And the distant sound of my dad's crackling bonfire.
I can hear the gasping wind.
I can feel the swishing of the leaves tickling my chin.
I can hear the grass swaying forwards and backwards,
As I crunch my feet through the soft and cushiony grass.
I'm very sorry to say but this poem must end now,
As I hear my mum calling me for tea!

Billy Meneer (9)
Gorran Primary School, St Austell

The Blitz

Through the gateway
Into the world
I'm sensing it's coming
I know it's coming
Down to Earth
From the heavens above
Tick-tock, tick-tock!

Dragons swooping
Men standing
It's coming so
I know it
Grit falling down my neck
Cloud morphing blood red
They're not the only one

Tick-tock, tick-tock
I know it's coming
I can see it
I know it's coming

Boom!

Anna Horigan (10)
Gwinear Community Primary School, Hayle

The Blitz

Something stirring, no one knows.
The build-up, everything froze.
Will it be today or will it be tomorrow?
I don't want it to be the day of sorrow!
Boom! The roar began, people running side to side.
I think it's time to hide . . .

In the morning it went away.
The musty feeling there to stay.
Bombs still activated.
Children evacuated.
The life of the town turned upside down!

Ben Skuse (10)
Gwinear Community Primary School, Hayle

The Blitz

Boom!
Roared the terrifying explosions.
I pounced out of my bed,
Eyes glared out of windows,
I could see some terrifying sights.
Everything wrecked,
Buildings rusted,
Rubble everywhere,
Dust flying,
Stairs cracking,
Like paper in a fire.
I ran to the door,
I slowly opened the door,
It creaked,
I walked outside,
I could taste the dust in my mouth,
It was revolting.
I could also feel the dust travel down my throat.
As I walked on, I could smell the unexploded bombs.
I shouted, 'Hello, is anyone there?'
It echoed but there was no answer.

Reave Kendall (10)
Gwinear Community Primary School, Hayle

The Blitz

Boom! A lion in battle
Sirens echoing around town.
Soldiers preparing for battle
Preparing for victory.

Crash! Houses falling
Spitfires and doodlebugs passing.
Soldiers shooting
People falling.

Bang! Factories blowing up
Anderson shelters falling down.
The night's over, the day begins
The smell of smoke and dustbins.

Screech! People worried
Dry throats!
Children leaving, being evacuated
In cars and boats.

People picking up bricks
Like the smell of sewage and bonfire.
The war is over, Britain wins!

Dalian Paul (9)
Gwinear Community Primary School, Hayle

Noisy Farm

Jacket potatoes groan
Cheese screams
Baked beans bubble
And sausages snort.

Cake whispers
And custard sighs
Jelly wobbles
In a bowl.

Blackberries squish
Apples crunch
Oranges squish
And stomach rumbles!

Charlotte Booker (7)
Jacobstow Community Primary School, Bude

Noisy Farm

Beans pop
Runner beans rip
Potatoes thump
Roast duck quacks.

Blackberries squelch
And bacon snuffles
Chicken chirps
In juicy gravy.

Sausages sizzle
Chips plop
Carrots crunch
And stomach rumbles!

Jack Biggs (7)
Jacobstow Community Primary School, Bude

The Noisy Farm

Bacon snuffles
Sausages oink
Milk moos
And cabbages flap.

Eggs cluck
And chicken chirps
Apples rustle
In a pie.

Melons pound
Oranges burst
Blackberries squelch
And stomach rumbles!

Sabrina Harris (8)
Jacobstow Community Primary School, Bude

Noisy Farm

Bacon snaps
Crunch, crunch
Runner beans pop
And celery rustles

Apples squelch
And blackberries bubble
With creamy custard
In a crumble.

Milk moos
In the bottle
Strawberries and cream
And stomach rumbles!

Frank Barriball (8)
Jacobstow Community Primary School, Bude

Noisy Farm

Sausages oink
Lettuce cracks
Celery snaps
And roast duck quacks.

Bacon snuffles
And runner beans rip
Cabbages flap
And potatoes flip.

Carrots crunch
Tomatoes squeal
Burgers stomp
And stomach grumbles!

Christopher Turner (7)
Jacobstow Community Primary School, Bude

Noisy Farm

Peas pop
Lettuce cracks
Sausages oink
And celery snaps.

Burgers stamp
And grapes tinkle
Bacon snuffles
In a pan.

Milk moos
Potatoes thump
Carrots crunch
And stomach rumbles . . . !

Molly Nutt (8)
Jacobstow Community Primary School, Bude

Noisy Farm

Carrots crunch
Cabbage flaps
Lamb chops baa
And pears plop.

Bacon snuffles
And runner beans rip
Chicken chirps
In juicy gravy.

Blackberries burst
With a drop of lemon
Pineapple bops
And stomach rumbles.

Jodie Bowman (8)
Jacobstow Community Primary School, Bude

Noisy Farm

Celery crunches
Potatoes thump
Apples rustle
And runner beans rip.

Milk moos
And carrots crunch
Celery snaps
In a bunch.

Peas pop
Cabbage flaps
Orange bursts
And stomach rumbles!

Chloe Tilley (8)
Jacobstow Community Primary School, Bude

The Noisy Farm

Carrots crunch
Potatoes thump
Roast duck quacks
And cabbage flaps.

Peas pop
And runner beans rip
Blackberries rumble
In a fruit crumble.

Apples rustle
Pears tussle
Peaches grumble
And a stomach rumbles.

Sean Cummins (8)
Jacobstow Community Primary School, Bude

Noisy Farm

Grapes tinkle
Pears plop
Apples rustle
And pineapple bops.

Bacon snuffles
And sausages splutter
Blackberries squelch
In blackberry pie.

Blackberries squish
With a scent of lemon
Oranges burst
And stomach rumbles!

Lucy Stevens (8)
Jacobstow Community Primary School, Bude

The Noisy Farm

Bacon snuffles
Eggs cluck
Carrots crunch
Peas pop.

Blackberries bubble
In juicy crumble
Milk moos and maas
Apples crunch in crusty pie.

Apples rustle
Grapes tinkle
Oranges burst
And stomach rumbles!

Thomas Turner (7)
Jacobstow Community Primary School, Bude

Noisy Farm

Carrots crunch
Lettuce snaps
Bacon snuffles
And runner beans crack.

Pineapple bops
And peas pop
Blackberries grumble
In blackberry crumble.

Lamb chops baa
Gravy tumbles
Roast duck quacks
Stomach rumbles!

Will Johnson (8)
Jacobstow Community Primary School, Bude

Pandas

Pandas are endangered
In trouble and afraid
Hunters of the forest
Look at what you've made!

There used to be a million
Wandering round the land
Come on killers, give 'em a break
They need a helping hand!

So save all of those pandas
All snuggled up and curled
Hunters, I am begging you
Let's make a better world!

Katie Devon Dymond (10)
Landulph Primary School, Saltash

The White Desert

Mist like liquid nitrogen,
Footsteps crack, crunch,
The fog climbing over you,
The cold biting,
Brain freezing.
A wispy, clear light,
A white desert,
Delicate droplets,
Unique flakes of rain,
Gently sinking snow,
Fatal coldness,
Freezing.

Joe Davey (10)
Lapford CP School, Crediton

The Bright Circle

As the bright circle rises,
It shines over the valley and the hills, the village,
It brightens up everyone's day.
The children play in the bright circle.
It brightens the sky blue,
It shines over the Earth,
Shining like a light bulb.
It goes many colours
When it is slowly going down like a bird.
It is made out of a big star.
It shines like a star.
It shines brightly.
It hangs from the sky
Like a circle hanging on a line.

Lesley Boatfield (10)
Lapford CP School, Crediton

Silent Breeze

The trees beside are green and tall,
A roaring blue line goes through the town.
Riding bikes and stopping for picnics
To have a little peer at it.
When the moon shines on,
The children watch it and
Some gaze at it all day through their windows.
The birds sing sweetly in the willow tree
And wake the children up at morning time.
The children rush downstairs
To go and see the silent breeze.

Megan Campbell Glover (9)
Lapford CP School, Crediton

The Morning Sun

In the morning it is bright.
You are sleeping peacefully in your bed,
You hear dogs howling noisily,
You can see it in your dreams.
At dawn where cats sing,
You can hear everything.

You think, lying in your cosy bed,
What on Earth is that?
A glowing semi-circle in the dark blue sky,
Glistening in the moonlight.
You go downstairs to have a cup of tea.
You wonder what you can see.

You tell everyone,
You take a picture,
It is beautiful.
It's fading fast,
Hurry up, it's going,
Quick before it goes.
Now it is gone,
The bright shiny circle has shone.

Georgia Youll (9)
Lapford CP School, Crediton

A Sinking Ball

Going down as it gets dark,
Everywhere else,
Lovely, bright, sinking,
Always goes down in other parts.
It goes down when it sleeps
Every day.
Everyone knows it's the biggest . . .
Star in the world.

Abbie Billings (10)
Lapford CP School, Crediton

Orange Ball Rising

The bright orange ball is rising gradually
Into the morning air.
I watched it go up
While I lay in my bed.

When I got up
It was still there,
Hanging lightly on an invisible string,
Right up in the now clear air.

I asked my extremely tired mum,
'Why does it rise?
Such a wonderful sight
Has come to my eyes.'

When I awoke the next day
It was gradually going up.
I watched it rise
And it looked much better than yesterday.

Kyle Tagg (9)
Lapford CP School, Crediton

White Space

I'm cold, dark but exciting.
I make it rain white cold shapes.
Halfway through me a joyous
Celebration is made.
Children have the time of their lives.
It's a nightmare in the mornings
To start the reluctant cars.
Millions of clouds join to make one mother cloud.
Animals have to collect food to stow away.
What am I?
Lakes will be frozen sculptures,
Bareness stands still and quiet on the ground.

Aaron Alcock (10)
Lapford CP School, Crediton

There's Something In The Ground

In the ground there is a great brown stick
With bright green dots on top.
Yummy round spheres hang from this tree,
Lots of brown twigs come out of this funny-looking object.
When this large brown stick is taller,
I might know what it is,
But for now I'll leave it to grow . . .

When I returned, the huge red spheres
Where I had been before, were slowly turning green.
The enormous stick was now taller than me.
The emerald-green dots were taller than my finger.
I could stay there all day . . .

I had to show somebody quickly.
I ran home impatiently to tell my mum,
But she said she would come tomorrow,
So I had to wait.

The next day she came.
It was even taller than my mum.
All the red, round orbs had
Fallen on the ground.
She took a picture for
The next time it comes around.

Katie Penny (9)
Lapford CP School, Crediton

Black Cover Shields The Sphere

A black sheet falls over me
And a white circle is appearing.
Gradually, small covers of glittering silver
Shine across my eyes.
I stare up above me
And there I see a beautiful vision.
I can't believe what I'm seeing
Because there isn't anything alike.
I sit impatiently and wait for a difference,
But nothing has happened since.
I have been here for long hours now,
But nothing's happened,
Not even a glint . . .

I'm thirsty and so hungry and I'm reluctant to go back in,
In case anything happens to the sheet of black
So I miss it.
I need to go inside and I know
That I would come back,
But as soon as I got in,
Everything went black,
Then I heard a sudden sound.
I woke up with a jump,
But then I saw it was light again,
And the sound was just my mum.

Louise Sibthorpe (8)
Lapford CP School, Crediton

Christmas

A lovely surprise,
Children enjoy it,
Get lots of presents,
Excitedly get ready for bed,
Can't get to sleep,
Hovering around the tree,
Listening to bells ringing,
Twisting and turning
Through the night.

It sometimes snows.
You can have a roast dinner,
Spend time with family,
Have lots of fun.
Children play with
Their new toys.

It's sad at the end
But new toys are fun,
I like to play with them.
It goes fast . . .
Too fast.

Sasha Moyes (8)
Lapford CP School, Crediton

Scrunchy, Scrunchy

Scrunchy, scrunchy, crunchy, crunch,
Down they plunge, millions still up,
All up high in a bunch.
Really peaceful until the wind blows.

They all fall off suddenly as winter comes.
Birds nest very close,
Weigh them all, lots of tones.
Scrunchy, scrunchy, crunch, crunch.

Ashley Cann (9)
Lapford CP School, Crediton

Dripping Water

The humid greenness loves
And the hotness burns,
The tall trees hang
And water falls,
Splashing everywhere,
Rustling leaves,
Howling like agonised wolves,
Rocks tumbling
Down a cliff,
Chattering monkeys
Swinging on trees
And poisonous snakes
Slithering sinuously
In and out of tree trunks and rocks,
Hissing and squeaking.

Daniel Tucker (10)
Lapford CP School, Crediton

Silent Swoosh

It goes swish, swoosh, swish, swoosh,
The trees beside it are green and tall.
People like to stop and watch the
Swish, swoosh, swish, swoosh.
When the wind comes it clatters
And falls against the tree, swish, swoosh.
All at once the children contemplate
Out of the window at the swish, swoosh.

All at once they rush downstairs
To take a look at the
Swish, swoosh, swish, swoosh.
They stare. The children always like it
When it goes swish, swoosh, swish, swoosh.

Amy Wood (8)
Lapford CP School, Crediton

A Yellow Stalk

Starts down small
And starts to grow.
Growing tall, as it
Grows a yellowy colour.

Sharp and spiky,
Tall and thin.
Getting taller and
Growing some grain.

In autumn it will
Be harvested,
Ready to make things.

It can be made
Into a lot of things,
One of them
Is bread.

Dylan May (8)
Lapford CP School, Crediton

The Big Green

The big green.
Lots of green-coloured balls
With long brown legs.
Very quiet, lots of sounds,
A dangerous place for a duck.
Not a place to play hide-and-seek.
Not such a good idea
To go hunting it.
Lots of horrible creatures and
No place to play and hide!

Sebastian Hepworth (9)
Lapford CP School, Crediton

The Pony That Nearly Got Caught

Her fur is as fluffy as a pillow,
Her eyes are like shiny buttons,
Hair tail is long and soft,
Her long pointy ears are like thorns.
Galloping through the moonlit woods,
The dry spinning leaves on the huge trees are waving
As she gallops past,
Neighing, neighing, neighing.
As she goes through the wood,
Birds fly out of the dry-leaved trees.
A frog leaps out of a pond.
Ding-dong, ding-dong, ding-dong,
The bells of the church are going off.
She hears people coming and
Some dogs barking, trying to catch her.
She runs away from the dogs and the people.

Jessica Burrows (9)
Lapford CP School, Crediton

That Pitter-Patter

A rainforest thing with grace and beauty
Shatters like crystals from the cliff,
Smashes below in all the white,
People come to admire this sight.
The rocks break the white beauty to bits
And the sound of raindrops goes pitter-patter from the sky,
Like snowdrops, nothing as cold,
Shatters this world that you can't hold.
It gleams over the edge of the cliff
And sprays everything in sight with white.
Wow, what a sight!

Christian Rushbrooke (9)
Lapford CP School, Crediton

What Am I?

Two-wheeler,
Three-gearer,
Scramble racer,
Mud slinger,
Water splasher,
Wow speeder,
Two times crasher.

Ryan Haynes (7)
Lapford CP School, Crediton

Pony

Loud neigher,
Feet clanger,
Wonderful rider,
Hay muncher,
Door slammer,
Good catcher,
High rearer,
It's a pony!

Rachael Powell (8)
Lapford CP School, Crediton

Climbing Sphere

It is as dark as coal for a while
Then gradually . . . gradually . . . gradually,
A burning ball of bright orange
Climbs a ladder for everyone to see.

It wakes everyone up,
And it gleams on you all day,
Until darkness wins the battle.

Joshua Lambert (10)
Lapford CP School, Crediton

Apollo In His Flaming Chariot

Apollo in his flaming chariot
Rides along the gold road.
When he's at the start it's dim,
In the middle it's bright,
And at the end it's beautiful.
As Apollo sets off from Olympus
He waves goodbye to Zeus
And as he speeds along,
He calls out to beautiful ladies
Attracted to his handsome body.
When he arrives back at Mount Olympus,
The Greek gods yell.
He has done another day of work
And made the crops grow well.

Jake Lewis (7)
Lapford CP School, Crediton

Untitled

I have very shiny wheels,
My engine is noisy and powerful,
Quick and fast,
As black as the night sky.

At the starting position, engines revving,
Whoosh! Off we go,
Zooming down the race track.
I'm first!
Quick, keep going,
They're catching up!

Jake Moyes (7)
Lapford CP School, Crediton

A Seaside Poem

There are fish living in me,
You can listen from a shell.
Everyone goes snorkeling in me.
On a hot day people come here.

I am sandy.
At night I'm rough, in the morning I'm calm.
Waves bash against the rocks.
I'm a sand collector,
I have jewels in me.
The moon reflects on me.

James Birtwistle (7)
Lapford CP School, Crediton

Unicorns

Purple eyes twinkling in the moonlight,
Sharp horn like a rhino's,
Pink mane and tail as soft as a fluffy cloud.

Flying through Magic Cloud Land,
Magic dust everywhere,
Tail floating gracefully in the air.

Chattering to a unicorn,
'What is that?'
Sharp ear behind a cloud.
Shadow of a figure.
'It's a weasel - fly, fly!'

Autumn Moxham (8)
Lapford CP School, Crediton

Dragons

A scaly back,
Long, pointy tail,
Lives in a dark, gloomy cave.
It blows lots of fire,
You will see a petrifying creature.

Ginormous flapping wings,
It likes to catch princesses.
Never friendly,
Most people hate them.
Only brave people fight them.

Ellie Poole (7)
Lapford CP School, Crediton

A Bird Near To Death

Thick brown feathers,
Piercing eyes focused on its prey,
Shining yellow beak,
Claws as sharp as a shark's tooth.

Squawking, squawking, squawking,
Flying through the night sky,
Wings ready for take-off,
Prey, watch out!

Bang, gunfire,
The bird squawks frantically,
Rocks fall, slight chance of death.

Jack Bastin (8)
Lapford CP School, Crediton

A Sinking Orb

A coloured ball falls from above,
It's been there all day
But now it's gone.
It will turn to another colour in a moment.

It has many a colour inside it,
It makes the people smile,
It covers the world
With its big smile.

Matthew Boddy (8)
Lapford CP School, Crediton

Death's Rotting Hand

She was there one minute, and not the next,
Lost, gone, never seen again.
She was snatched from our loving arms
And fell into the scabbed, rotting hands.

Sadly those hands were not ours
And her body was no more,
Only to be found by those who do not seek it.
I hope it did not hurt.

I miss her; I miss her a lot.
Every night I look at the sky,
Trying to find her single star,
For those hands belonged to death,
And Emma is at rest.

Jocelin Guy (10)
Lipson Vale Primary School, Plymouth

After School Clubs

When we go to after school clubs,
The teachers all go home.
Mr Smith goes home in his Bentley
And the head teacher's all alone.

Some kids do their cycling proficiency,
Some of them go to netball,
But there's always mayhem in the playground
When Josh wrecks the climbing wall.

But the best club of all
That's been seen by me
Is Sir's fantastic sports club:
Tag rugby!

Lawrence Cooper (10)
Lipson Vale Primary School, Plymouth

Five Lazy Teachers
(Inspired by 'Ten Naughty Schoolboys' by A A Milne)

Five lazy teachers looking at the door,
One remembered his oven and then there were four.

Four lazy teachers, one needed a pee!
So he went to the toilet and then there were three.

Three lazy teachers all looking blue,
One puked on the floor and then there were two.

Two lazy teachers, both really dumb,
One walked into the door and then there was one.

One lazy teacher having lots of fun,
He walked off home and then there was *none!*

Darren Ford (10)
Lipson Vale Primary School, Plymouth

A Place Close To My Heart

I go there on my birthday,
When the clock strikes noon,
Have a little fun and Mum has a glass of wine too!
As the sun goes down
I walk through the glass double doors
To the land outside.
I sit on the wall
And look at the reflection of the moon
In the glimmering water.
When I was younger they used to tell me
There was a sea monster,
The sea monster of beauty.

Renée Barry (10)
Lipson Vale Primary School, Plymouth

Mothers

Gentle, kind and beautiful creatures that
Were sent from Heaven above!
Mothers, mothers, pretty and sweet,
They clean up after us all our lives.
They're the ones that fluff up our pillows
And kiss us goodnight.
We respect our mothers every stage of our lives.
The smell of their perfume and powder,
All the make-up they wear,
The reassuring scent of their hair.
Our mothers are our best friends.

Charlotte Benwell (10)
Lipson Vale Primary School, Plymouth

School Days

The school days are really long.
I always start with my alarm,
Our wake up, shake up, it's just wrong
That we can't be in our pyjamas.

We don't do much art
And we can't get out (much),
So we have to look smart and be smart,
Then the teachers shout!

In maths we do our times tables backwards,
That's so not the way!
They are really hard.
This is not a normal school day!

Danielle Green (10)
Lipson Vale Primary School, Plymouth

Mental Maths

Another morning of mental maths.
'Oh what did you say, Sir?' shouted the class in laughs.
'Today,' said Sir excitedly, 'is the 0.7 and back.'
'Hooray,' groaned the class with an enthusiastic lack.

'After that, it's fraction improper we are doing today.'
Sir would pay anything for us to do it his way.
Staring at the whiteboard with fifths on
At the bottom, a five on the top of a one.

We are sitting in our chairs waiting for the sound
Of the glorious bell, letting us go into the playground.
As we think that, mind-reading Sir can tell,
And within the next ten seconds, there goes the bell.

Lucas Woodbridge (11)
Lipson Vale Primary School, Plymouth

Through The Staffroom

(Inspired by 'Ten Naughty Schoolboys' by A A Milne)

Ten grumpy teachers never noticed the time,
One went back to class and then there were nine.

Nine grumpy teachers were asked out for a date,
One agreed to do it and then there were eight.

Eight grumpy teachers made a trip to Heaven,
One never made it and then there were seven.

Seven grumpy teachers went to pick up sticks,
One found the Big Bad Wolf and then there were six.

Six grumpy teachers were about to be eaten alive,
One got ripped by a bone and then there were five.

Five grumpy teachers broke the ancient law,
One got cursed by a mummy and then there were four.

Four grumpy teachers had to find the biggest bee,
One got stung by his and then there were three.

Three grumpy teachers jumped out and shouted, *'Boo!'*
One got scared to death and then there were two.

Two grumpy teachers didn't have any fun,
One got bored stiff and then there was one.

One grumpy teacher saw his all-time hero,
He went off to join him and then there was zero.

Hannah Humphries (10)
Lipson Vale Primary School, Plymouth

World Peace

Why can't we just have world peace?
To have friends, not foes please!
It would be perfect . . .
But who would make it happen?
The person who can make it happen . . .
Please, please, please make it happen.

Amber Stearman (10)
Lipson Vale Primary School, Plymouth

Through The Classroom Door

(Inspired by 'Ten Naughty Schoolboys' by A A Milne)

Ten sleepy children slumped in their seats at playtime,
One remembered to ring the bell then there were nine.

Nine sleepy children with one best mate,
One went off to the sweetshop then there were eight.

Eight sleepy children thinking of chocolate heaven,
One went off to buy a bar then there were seven.

Seven sleepy children, one got in a fix,
He was rushed to hospital then there were six.

Six sleepy children, one suddenly felt alive,
So he went to play with his friends then there were five.

Five sleepy children, one ten feet tall,
He crashed into a teacher then there were four.

Four sleepy children, one was desperate for a wee,
He went off to the toilet then there were three.

Three sleepy children, one caught the flu,
He went home then there were two.

Heidi Steer (10)
Lipson Vale Primary School, Plymouth

Special Friendship

If you have a friendship, value it,
It is a very special thing to have.
If I ever lose it, I will cry for days,
So I make the most of it.

My friends are very special,
If one of them got hurt,
I would be there to support them
And be there every minute of the day.

Danielle English (11)
Lipson Vale Primary School, Plymouth

My Hamster

You were my pet, my friend,
My one and only hamster,
Until the cat of death
Pierced its teeth upon your flesh.
That was the end of you.
Nothing left, just your blood on my bed.
Now you are dead.

Kana Tachibana-Doyle (10)
Lipson Vale Primary School, Plymouth

My Cat

My cat, my friend, my world,
So energetic and playful,
Follows me on the prowl, having so much fun,
A unique creature, the best pet,
As sweet as rose petals falling delicately to the ground.
You make me glad, Rosie!

Jenny Cox (11)
Lipson Vale Primary School, Plymouth

Who Is It?

DIY worker,
Rugby watcher,
Motorbike maker,
Dinner hater,
Funny singer,
Chocolate eater,
My saviour,
Who is it?
My dad.

Katie Cook (10)
Lipson Vale Primary School, Plymouth

What Am I?

Round-object,
Good-flyer,
Air-filler,
Foot-smacker,
Ground-rubber,
Padded-lover,
Net-scorer.
What am I?
A football!

Jacob Warner (11)
Lipson Vale Primary School, Plymouth

Tigers

Orange as carrots with black stripes,
Hiding in the grass,
Creeping, crawling, looking for prey.

Please don't shoot me for money and food,
Tiger, soon there will be only two.

Jasmine Hancock (10)
Lipson Vale Primary School, Plymouth

Who Am I?

A lettuce muncher,
A slow walker,
A shelled creature,
Nature's tank!
A fast swimmer,
Well hidden,
Munch, munch!
Who am I?
A tortoise.

Ryan Finn (11)
Lipson Vale Primary School, Plymouth

Johnny Wilkinson

One swift kick could end it all,
But only if you hit the ball.
You are the one to end it all.

You wear the kit that makes you proud,
Only in front of a cheering crowd.

Your number ten is like your friend
Because it's the only number that blends.

As you kick the ball straight through,
All the grinning teeth look at you.

So one swift kick could end it all,
But only if you hit the ball.

Curtis Hallett (11)
Lipson Vale Primary School, Plymouth

Perfect Pets

Fluffy, furry and cute,
Tall and small as well,
Warm and comforting,
Cuddle and don't let go.

Cats, dogs and rabbits,
Hamsters and gerbils too,
Just so cuddly,
Just so tiny,

My pets are the best!

Samantha Townsend (10)
Lipson Vale Primary School, Plymouth

Five Lazy Children

(Inspired by 'Ten Naughty Schoolboys' by A A Milne)

Five lazy children staring at the open door,
One made a slow getaway then there were four.

Four lazy children, one needed a wee,
He went to the toilet then there were three.

Three lazy children, one was fairly new,
One had a nosebleed and then there were two.

Two lazy children, both having fun,
One hurt his leg and then there was one.

One lazy child, thinking he was a hero,
He blasted off into space and then there were zero.

Aimée Ruffle (10)
Lipson Vale Primary School, Plymouth

What Am I?

Face-licker,
Jumper-upper,
Good-hugger,
Best-stroker,
Tail-wagger,
Loud-barker,
Cat-hater,
Rat-liker,
No biter.

Who am I?
A dog!

Bryony Butler (10)
Lipson Vale Primary School, Plymouth

Nightmare!

It rattles my window,
It bangs on the door,
It attacks my teddies
And it screams on the floor.

It makes creepy noises,
It bites all my jewels,
It murdered my doll
And breaks all the rules.

It sleeps in my cupboard with all my bears,
It eats all my sweets,
It falls down the stairs
And smells my mum's feet.

It screamed in my face,
It pulled on my hair,
Then whispered in my ear,
'It's just a *nightmare!*'

Elissia Roberts (10)
Marlborough Primary School, Falmouth

Don't Stand And Cry

Every day I look at the sky,
Wondering how birds can fly.
I never thought his day would come,
But that is why I am so glum.
We sat and though and cried awhile,
But then we thought of Grandad's smile.
So now he's gone, I won't forget,
But I still might be a little upset.

Olivia Morrison (10)
Marlborough Primary School, Falmouth

Young Writers - Little Laureates Poems From Devon & Cornwall

Shipwreck Exploring

The boat so rusty,
We are all so trusty,
Come with me and see
The deep blue sea.
There we see a battered sail,
Then we see a blue whale.

Look, a shark so horrible and grim,
A shadow, ouch! What's that thing?
In a clam I see some pearls,
Then I see a mermaid's wonderful curls.
The shipwreck destroyed, it seems so bad,
It makes me feel so sad.

The shipwreck's rope, all torn and tattered,
It must have been really battered.
We go down into the deep,
We go down sixty feet.
Look, a fish made of jelly,
I'd hate to have him in my belly!

Isabel Stephens (10)
Mount Charles Primary School, St Austell

My Family

I have a mum and a dad,
And I have a sister who makes me glad.
We have a dog who is very silly,
He's big and black and we call him Billy.

We live together in our home,
I'm so lucky that I'm not alone.
I play on the swings and bikes too,
And I chase my dog if he gets my shoe.

Rosie Mingo (7)
Mount Charles Primary School, St Austell

My Cat Poem

My cats are cute,
They like to hide in my wellie boot.
They love to climb and play
And they also like to be on their way,
But they don't always obey.
They are cute and cuddly, oh yes,
They are my little pooches and
I like them best.
Just then Misty kissed me
And Maisy is tired as usual.
I know she is a baby
But I just want to play.
I really, really want to play,
But all they do now is run away.
I don't know why I bother
But I guess they are only babies
And I guess they are sort of cute
When they want to be.
But now their claws are getting sharper,
I guess it's time to run with laughter.

Laura Holman (10)
Mount Charles Primary School, St Austell

School Work

English, maths,
ICT too,
Them all put together
Is great fun for you!
English is writing,
Maths is sums,
And the best of all
Are the teachers -
They're *fun!*

Charlie Retallick (9)
Mount Charles Primary School, St Austell

Ice Is Nice!

Ice is nice,
It's clear as crystal,
White as winter.

In the snow, paw prints show,
Birds are singing in the early morning,
Presents wrapped under the Christmas tree.

Ice is nice,
It's clear as crystal,
White as winter.

Santa comes down the chimney,
Spilling soot all over the floor,
Sharing his joyfulness.

Ice is nice,
It's clear as crystal,
White as winter.

Thea Rowley (9)
Mount Charles Primary School, St Austell

Mud Maid

Beacon's path full of twisted trees,
Soft, spongy moss as you walk in New Zealand.
Mud Maid is sleepy while children make noise,
Ghostly grey lady's place.
The fountain drips with glittery water,
Mud Maid is sleepy while children make noise,
Ghostly grey lady's place.
Beacon's path full of twisted trees,
Soft, spongy moss as you walk in New Zealand,
The fountain drips with glittery water.

Jessica Trahair (9)
Mount Charles Primary School, St Austell

Beetle

Beetle, beetle,
Scuttle along,
Beetle, beetle
Don't lollop along.
Beetle, beetle,
Mind my foot,
Beetle, beetle,
Don't do that beat with your feet.
Beetle, beetle,
Hide away,
Beetle, beetle,
I'll see you another day.
Beetle, beetle,
Be my friend,
Beetle, beetle,
That will have to be the end.

Daniel Watkins (7)
Mount Charles Primary School, St Austell

Fire

The amber fire, it burns so bright,
I sit beside it night by night.
My cat, called Fang, he likes to lie
And watch the world go by and by.

It's so very cold outside today,
So in I come by the fire to lay.
My cat, Fang, comes by my side
And here we stay and both reside.

I feel I want to sleep,
I look at Fang but he's asleep.
My dad, he takes me up to bed,
I'm very tired, I feel like lead.

Amber Dumbleton (10)
Mount Charles Primary School, St Austell

Haunted Hallowe'en

Step in through the rusty gates
Be quiet as a mouse,
Tiptoe to the creepy door
Inside the haunted house.

I am the monster hiding under your bed,
Teeth so sharp and eyes going red.
I am the monster hiding under your stairs,
Snakes as fingers and spiders in my hair.

In the kitchen there's a witch
Making slug and spider stew,
If you dare come, have a peek,
But beware, she can get you!

Tiptoe through the rusty gates,
Be quiet as a mouse,
But don't let them hear you
Escape the haunted house!

Jayd Cloughton-Kehoe (10)
Mount Charles Primary School, St Austell

A Poem At The Seaside

I know where the seaside is,
I know it very well,
It is where the sea crashes against the rocks.
It is where the seagulls swoop round in the sky,
It is where the sand is soft and is made into sandcastles,
It is where you can splash around in the sea and have fun,
It is where the sand blows in your face,
It is where you can have a picnic,
It is where the fish swim in the sea,
It is where the crabs crawl in the rock pools,
It is where the seaweed sways.
That is where the seaside is.

Bryher Semonin (7)
Mount Charles Primary School, St Austell

The Journey To Atlantis

Splash . . . shhhh.

All aboard,
Save me now,
We're going on a ride,
A big ride,
A really big ride,
Splash . . . shhhh.
We're in the water,
We're twisting and turning,
What's that?
Mermaid?
Serpent?
'Ha, ha, ha,' a water witch screams,
Lunging towards us.
Suddenly
We are going up,
Doors swing open and . . . daylight.
We're plunging down, down, down,
Splash . . . shhhh.
Water spray everywhere,
Hold on,
Up again, higher and higher,
Twisting sharply at the top
Then plummeting down and down and down.
Splash . . . shhhh.

Carla Aldington (9)
Mount Charles Primary School, St Austell

Ducks

D ucks go *quack* as they swim,
U nder water looking for food,
C ome and see them in the park,
K ing of the wild birds,
S cavenging for food.

Sophie Weedon (11)
Mount Charles Primary School, St Austell

Flower Paradise

Flower paradise
Has scarlet-red roses,
The bluest bluebells,
Sunny, sensational flowers,
Pretty pink tulips,
Little orange geraniums,
Fabulous fuchsias
And butter-coloured buttercups.

Florence Strookman (7)
Mount Charles Primary School, St Austell

Monkeys

I love monkeys, they are cool,
They are my favourite thing of all.
With their cheeky faces and funny grins,
They run around making a din.
Funky monkeys are the best,
I wish I could have one as a pet.

Katie Wenmouth (7)
Mount Charles Primary School, St Austell

I Am The Sea

I am the sea,
I am lovely and blue,
Boats come from all around
And squish me.
I hate it when children
Swim in me,
They hit me with their hands.
I hate it when they kick and splash me.
I wish I was safer so people wouldn't drown.

Danni Rickard (10)
Mount Charles Primary School, St Austell

Amazing Clothes

Warm woolly jumpers, all different colours,
Cosy knitted gloves, scarves and hats,
Coats of all different sizes,
Long coats, short coats, fluffy coats and soft coats.

Diamond, crystal, high-heeled boots,
Sequinned swirly dresses,
Sparkly jewelled sashes,
Glittering, shining bags.

Brightly-coloured beach towels,
Flower-patterned bikinis,
Sassy short skirts,
Fantastic flippy flip-flops,
Gorgeous, glamorous sunglasses,
Funky monkey beach bag.

Super shiny Wellingtons,
Bright, brilliant raincoats,
Big colourful umbrellas,
Dazzling, gleaming rain hats.

April Talbot (7)
Mount Charles Primary School, St Austell

I Like . . .

I like to sit beside the sea
And listen to the waves,
To feel the sand between my toes
And run through hidden caves!
To sit and watch the birds fly by
And crabs that swim in pools,
I like to sit beside the sea
On days I'm not in school!

Georgia Rawling (9)
Mount Charles Primary School, St Austell

My Chipmunks

My chipmunks are cute and cuddly,
They love to come out to play.
When they see me in the room,
They jump up and squeak, 'Hooray'.
I give them some nuts to calm them down
And they love to bury them far away.

I know they're only tiny
But I just want to play.
I check that they are OK every day
Because I know they're only young.
I just want to play.

I cuddle their fluffy bodies and stroke their bushy tails.
My chipmunks are so special to me in one particular way.
They are my favourite tiny animals to stroke all day.

Summer Williams (9)
Mount Charles Primary School, St Austell

Kittens

I wish I had a kitten,
All furry and so cute,
I would call him Archimedes
And love him all day long.

I wish I had a kitten,
All ginger and so sweet,
I'd cuddle and play with him,
Whenever he needed me.

Oh, I wish I had a kitten.

Rachel Pinder (7)
Mount Charles Primary School, St Austell

The Sweet Garden

The sweet garden
Has candyfloss clouds
And chocolate gates,
Coca-Cola lakes full of sugary-sour fish,
Don't forget ice cream trees
And gingerbread girls and boys,
Toffee swirl-flavoured roses,
Tulips of fizzy lollipops.

Teri Trevains (8)
Mount Charles Primary School, St Austell

Watching Fireworks

Fireworks bash, boom and pop,
In different shapes and colours.
Fireworks are beautiful,
So clap, clap, clap.
Fireworks bang,
Hit and boom.
Fireworks, *bang, bang, bang.*

Bernice Barnes (10)
Mount Charles Primary School, St Austell

The Jungle

'Oo-oo, ahh-ahh,' monkeys in the trees,
Hissing pythons playing with the bees.
A lion cub cutely playing on the floor,
First there was one, now there's more!
Leather-back turtles scrambling on the sand,
Then an eagle swoops to land.
Dolphins happily squeaking in the sea,
All of them wanting to play with me!
I like the jungle.

Milo Semonin (9)
Mount Charles Primary School, St Austell

Young Writers - Little Laureates Poems From Devon & Cornwall

Monkey Rhyming Poem

Monkeys swing from tree to tree,
Monkeys, why can't you come and play with me?
Monkeys eat bananas for tea,
Why can't they eat a chimpanzee?
Monkeys see me singing a song,
But they say it's all wrong.
Monkeys swing from tree to tree,
Can I have some tea?
Monkeys see me coming through,
They ask where am I going to?
I say I'm going down to the lake,
You must not make any mistakes.

Rositta Caesar (10)
Mount Charles Primary School, St Austell

The Sea

The sea is a baboon,
Grey and hungry,
His paws snatching for food,
His great jaws gnashing on the sand.

His tail lashing on the cliffs,
Taking the rocks off the shore,
His belly rising up and down as he breathes,
He lets out a mighty roar.

In the months of May and June,
The reeds don't make their reedy tune.
There is no noise on the beach,
Except the baboon's gentle screech.

Noah Semonin (10)
Mount Charles Primary School, St Austell

Weather, Weather, Weather

The Sun

The sun, it blobs across the sky leaving a shining light,
It's like a splatter of yellow paint,
As yellow as a tall and healthy primrose,
Shimmering, shining sun, cooking me like a sausage.

The Wind

The wind, wandering, whipping, wild wind, whispering to me,
It sweeps across my garden - until it notices me on the trampoline.
It's like a crafty fox after chickens on Old McDonald's farm.

The Rain

The rain, rushing, running, rampaging rain, rapping at my window.
It's like fireworks dropping down to Earth, only not as colourful.

Shanice Morrison (8)
Mount Street Primary School, Plymouth

My Weather Poem

The wind is like a huge snake as it coils around me.
The wind is like a whistle being blown softly.
The wind can be like a giant, ripping trees out of the ground.

The sun is like an enormous tomato on fire in the bright blue sky.
The sun is like a red boiling fireball as it creeps across the sky.
The sun is like a gigantic light bulb exploding in the sky.

Rain is like God as he tips a bucket of cold water on Earth.
Rain is like someone in Heaven watering his plants.
Rain is like the morning hose as it drenches you top to bottom.

Lucas Booker-Munoz (8)
Mount Street Primary School, Plymouth

My Weather Poem

The sun glitters in my eyes like gold.
The sun sizzles and lets off its colours.
The sun is shining over the whole world
By letting off its fireball.

The wind whistles through my hair
And whispers to me, telling me secrets.
The wind blows my hair into my face.
The wind takes my hair out of my face.

The clouds break into little pictures in the sky.
The clouds smile in the sky.
The clouds race across the sky.

Natalia Hempsall (8)
Mount Street Primary School, Plymouth

My Weather Poem

The wind flows and whistles through my hair
While I walk through the peaceful park.
The wind is fast like the speed of light.
The wind is wise like a wizard in his lair.
The sun blasts the green trees.
The rain drips and drops on my window sill.
The rain falls down with a silent splatter
On the smooth tarmac.
The sun is as bright as 200,000,000 light bulbs.
The light blue raindrops fall like a feather fluttering down.
The sun whispers like a mouse hiding from a cat.

Joseph Tiernan (9)
Mount Street Primary School, Plymouth

My Weather Poem

Clouds like candyfloss moving in the sky.
Clouds like cotton wool passing over my head.
Clouds like an enormous sheep.

Wind whispers to me.
The wind comes to my bedroom without a key.
The wind is as strong as a giant pulling the roof off a house.

Sparkling sun, shining and sizzling in the bright sky.
Sunshine like a bright golden ball.
The sun twinkles when I get up from bed and smiles at me.

Kamila Amer (9)
Mount Street Primary School, Plymouth

My Weather Poem

The sun sizzles sadly and quietly.
The sun sparkles, shimmers and shakes.
The sun smiles, glitters and is bright.

The clouds cluster, crashing and crumbling.
The clouds, graceful, shape-shifting and sliding.
The clouds race, float and fly.

The wind whispers wildly in my ear.
The wind wails wildly.
The wind wails, whispering sadly.

Lauren Kerry (8)
Mount Street Primary School, Plymouth

The Waterfall - Haiku

Moving waterfall,
Gushing, flowing very fast,
Dangerous and cold.

Katie Brown (9)
Mount Street Primary School, Plymouth

Colour Poem

Red is a very angry colour.
Orange is a lovely juicy colour.
Yellow is like a tall sunflower.
Green is a carpet of grass.
Blue is a bright summer sky.
Purple is the colour of my favourite book.
Black is a really haunting colour.
White is scary like a white, hairy ghost.

Heaven Fenn (8)
Mount Street Primary School, Plymouth

My Weather Poem

Clouds burst, it rains all across the sky.
The rain scatters across the sky just like a bird.
The sun shines like a golden key.
The sun sparkles as it comes through my window.
The sun is as hot as a blazing hot fireball
That is from another planet.
The wind can wake me up when I am sleeping.
The wind can rip off my wonderful coat.
The wind is cold and friendly.

Isabel Davies (8)
Mount Street Primary School, Plymouth

Tree - Haiku

One cold winter's night
In my garden a tree creaks.
The shadow scares me.

Corey Blackmore (10)
Mount Street Primary School, Plymouth

Waterfall

Diving in the water,
Bouncing on the rocks
Like a trampoline.
Crashing and bashing
Up against the wall,
Like the waterfall
Is chucking a
Big bucket of water
All over you.
It's like you
Are going in a
Freezing cold
Jacuzzi with
Fish swimming
Everywhere!

Emily McArthur (10)
Mount Street Primary School, Plymouth

My Weather Poem

The sun is like a huge yellow firework
Lighting up the sky.
The sun is like a bright yellow balloon
Floating high in the sky.
The sun is as hot as the Sahara Desert sands.
The wind is as strong as a giant
Knocking down houses.
The wind is as frosty as
Sitting in a freezer.
The wind is as tough as an
Elephant ready to charge.

Brandon Joll (9)
Mount Street Primary School, Plymouth

My Weather Poem

The Wind

The wind whistles as it ripped my coat off.
The wind whispers in my ear.
The wind winds like a critter in the desert.

The Sun

The sun shines like the desert sand.
The sun shimmers like a golden key.
The sun glows like a torch in the sky.

The Rain

The rain rushes rapidly on my face.
The rain dribbles on my window at home.
The rain rips through the clothes that you are wearing.

Travis Haydon (10)
Mount Street Primary School, Plymouth

A Cloud Is Like . . .

A cloud is part of a community,
They way they bond and pull together.

A cloud is always moving,
Always looking for a new place to settle.

A cloud has always got a friend,
When it moves, its friends move with it.

A cloud cruises across the sky
Like a person without a care.

A cloud is like a person crying
When he's sad.

Conner Mitchell (11)
Mount Street Primary School, Plymouth

My Weather Poem

Cloud

The cloud is as stupid as a clown, also I can see it.
The cloud is as annoying as a crazy frog, also I can hear it.
The cloud is as fluffy as candyfloss, also I can feel it.

Sun

The sun is as sunny as a soggy day and I feel it.
The sun is as steamy as a hot bath and I can feel it.
The sun is as yellow as the desert sand and I can see it.

Wind

The wind is as destructive as an army and I can see it.
The wind is as dangerous as a monster truck and I can feel it.
The wind is following the breeze like a butterfly in the sky and
I can hear it.

Cameron Moule (9)
Mount Street Primary School, Plymouth

My Weather Poem

The wind is as fast as a cheetah catching its prey.
The sun glows across the sea like a torch at night shining on the sea.
The rain is as boring as a pig.
The clouds are as white as a beautiful white swan.
The wind is as cold as an ice cube.
The sun is as hot as a big fire.
The clouds float across the sky like a graceful swan.
The wind is as calm as a bird.

Michael Pascoe (8)
Mount Street Primary School, Plymouth

My Weather Poem

Wind

The wandering wind whistles and whispers to my face.
The wind flows like a graceful swan on the pond.
The wind blows like a wild, destructive tiger.

Sun

The sun shines brightly like a golden key.
The sun blazes through the sky like a red fireball.
The sun shifts slowly like a slithery slug.

Cloud

The cloud is fluffy and soft like candyfloss.
The cloud sways slowly like the waves of the sea.
The cloud is so fluffy, like a rabbit's tail.

Fahad (8)
Mount Street Primary School, Plymouth

My Weather Poem

The sun shines, spectacular like gleaming gold.
The sun blazes across the bright blue sky.
The sun floats across the sky like a graceful swan.

The cloud whisks across the bright blue sky.
The cloud moves across the sky like a graceful swan.
The cloud floats across the graceful sky.

The rain floats right through me.
The rain slowly drips on me.
The rain gathers in a weird shape.

Bethany Pennington (8)
Mount Street Primary School, Plymouth

Rainy Days - Cinquain

Drip, drip,
Drops on your skin
On a wet, rainy day
Puddles are made on the wet ground
Splash! Splash!

Alisha Pennington (10)
Mount Street Primary School, Plymouth

Fire - Haiku

Fire is piping hot,
When it goes out it leaves ash.
Fire is dangerous.

Connor Mitchell (10)
Mount Street Primary School, Plymouth

The Sea And Me - Cinquain

The waves
Of the ocean
Stroking my hair swiftly,
Making me feel very relaxed,
Shining.

Tanaka Mudimu Jimalo (10)
Mount Street Primary School, Plymouth

What Am I? - Cinquain

Shiny
In the night sky,
Glittering and sparkling,
Dark, cold, distant light is twinkling
Silver.

Florence Sullivan (9)
Mount Street Primary School, Plymouth

The Fiery Depths Of A Volcano - Cinquain

Burning,
Destroying you,
Creating a monster
More deadly than a beam of death,
Sparkling.

Isaac Davies (9)
Mount Street Primary School, Plymouth

The Burning Flame - Cinquain

Dreadful,
Fear and killing,
Bubbling, also deadly,
Stirring and burning, destructive,
Raging.

Richard Sharman (11)
Mount Street Primary School, Plymouth

Flowers - Haiku

Flowers popping, bang,
Striking sunny bold morning,
Sparking, shooting, bold.

Kyah Brooks (9)
Mount Street Primary School, Plymouth

The Tree - Cinquain

Swaying,
Branches blowing,
Seeing leaves falling off,
Old oak trees swaying in the breeze,
Magic.

Jake Rout (10)
Mount Street Primary School, Plymouth

My Weather Poem

The clouds clatter my face together.
The clouds are good at making pictures.
The clouds are as cold as ice.

The sun sparkles in my bedroom window.
The sun shimmers at my face brightly.
The sun is has hot as a blazing hot fire.

The wind is as wild as a lion.
The wind wanders through my hair.
The wind whistles through my hair like a tornado.

Katie Smyth (8)
Mount Street Primary School, Plymouth

My Weather Poem

The wind mysteriously blew in the sky.
The wind raced all clouds like thunder.
The wind whistled from the window like a little bug.

The clouds floated like a soft bed.
The clouds tasted like candyfloss.
The clouds floated like white angels.

The sun shone in the sky like lightning.
The sun shone in the sky like a gold key.

The rain rained so harshly that the trees fell down.
The rain poured like a drink of water.
The rain fell so hard that it washed all the leaves away.

Liga Ozolina (9)
Mount Street Primary School, Plymouth

Fear - Cinquain

'Eeyore'
Went the donkey
Running around in fear
Because it saw a black python.
Donkey.

Tino Mwadeyi (10)
Mount Street Primary School, Plymouth

Lightning - Cinquain

Clash! Clash!
I lie in bed.
'Please can I have a look?'
'No,' said Mum, 'for it is only
Lightning.'

Elisabeth Temlett-Dixon (10)
Mount Street Primary School, Plymouth

Tidal Wave - Haiku

Shimmering, spitting,
Rushing down the lane quickly,
It races forward.

Jacob Foran (10)
Mount Street Primary School, Plymouth

My Weather Poem

The wind is wavy like a huge fan.
The wind is running like a racing car.
The wind is gentle like it is a scent.

The sun is boiling like a hot fireplace.
The sun is a gas ball that's like a gas station.
The sun is as yellow as a yellow banana.

The cloud is as flexible as a sponge.
The cloud is as white as a swan.
The cloud is as light as a feather.

Bailey White (9)
Mount Street Primary School, Plymouth

Whales

How good it is to be free
Among my family and pod.
We talk with little squeaking noises,
Don't hook me with your rod.

I can be very gentle
Like a king, giant of the sea.
I bet that you wish
You could kiss and cuddle me.

I feel so smooth and soft.
I am as big as a bus.
Don't carve me up for rubbers
Because everyone's making a fuss.

Stop! Stop! You're polluting my home.
If you carry on, I'll be living alone.
All that rubbish: cans, bottles and even a comb.
You've killed me now, so everyone will moan.

Tanya Pearson & Molly Finch (9)
Newton Ferrers CE Primary School, Plymouth

Death Of The Dolphin

How good it is to fly
'Long the side of a fisherman's boat,
And then to swim around
Exploring others as they float.

How good to feel the waves'
Rough stroke against my shiny skin.
How bad to feel the tinge of fear
When nets I get caught in.

How horrible it is to glide,
Dying more each day.
How awful is my fate
That in my ocean I no longer play.

Joshua Eason (9) & Phoebe Rhead (10)
Newton Ferrers CE Primary School, Plymouth

Hear The Cry Of The Pilot Whale

Hear the cry of the pilot whale
Echoing through the mist.
Here come the Faroe Island villagers
Covering my blowhole with their fists.

The blood of all my pod
Makes the sea run deep, dark red,
And with all the pain I'm going through,
I give up and lower my head.

One last smell of the ocean,
One more feel of the sun,
One more breath of clean fresh air,
My time on this Earth is done.

Joshua Turner (8) & Jeremy Eason (9)
Newton Ferrers CE Primary School, Plymouth

More! More! More!

We need more holidays abroad
More oil from our rigs.
We want more waves for surfing
And some space to row our gigs.
We want another aquarium.
We want ten thousand fishing boats.
We want to build bigger submarines
For the navy to stay afloat.
More noise to dull dolphins' screams.
Watch more whales jumping in the sea.
More lipstick, soap and perfume.
It's all for me! Me! Me!

Can anybody hear us?
We need our open spaces,
We need to live here too,
We'd like to share your planet
If that's okay with you.
And oceans, food and sunlight,
And tangled bits of coral,
No nets that rise beyond the horizon,
We need our space to hunt our prey.
Leave us in privacy.
Please don't use the world up,
It's the only one we've got!

Erik Wilson (9), Aimee Burlinson & James Wall (10)
Newton Ferrers CE Primary School, Plymouth

Giants Of The Ocean

I'm a city boy. I was born in my pool.
Suddenly rushed into training school.

I'm a whale used for public shows.
They make me jump up and pose.

I dream of the ocean where my mum was born,
Where we could hunt our prey at the crack of dawn.

Fergus Carruthers (9) & Freddy Hillier (10)
Newton Ferrers CE Primary School, Plymouth

Whale

I am a friendly beast
Swimming through the waves.
Stop chasing me, stop killing me.

Like a deep sea diver
I plunge to the seabed.
Stop chasing me, stop killing me.

I am the king of the sea,
Swimming in the depths of the ocean.
Stop chasing me, stop killing me.

Like a giant hoover
I suck up krill.
Stop chasing me, stop killing me.

I migrate for hundreds of miles
To the feeding grounds.
Stop chasing me, stop killing me.

One day a fisherman said to me,
'You are the monster of the sea.'
But where are my brothers?
Stop chasing me, stop killing me.

Ben Harvey (8) & Ben King (10)
Newton Ferrers CE Primary School, Plymouth

Blue Stripe

Dolphins are so elegant
Flowing through the water.
Swirling, twirling, gracefully turning
Through the lashing waves.

If you do not save me,
I will do you no good.
You won't be able to ride on my back,
Glide through the sea, as you could.

Imogen Tarran (9)
Newton Ferrers CE Primary School, Plymouth

The Joyful Dolphin

How good it is to dive
Deep down among the fish.
And then to spend the day
Caught by a net, I did not wish.

How good it is to glide and jump,
Swimming near the shore.
Living on the coral reef
And exploring the sea floor.

Dashing through the waves,
Past the sparkle of the sea.
Gliding over other fish,
Swimming gracefully.

Nathan King (8) & Juliet Hepburn (9)
Newton Ferrers CE Primary School, Plymouth

Whales

I am as big as a bus,
As black as night.
Stop chasing me, stop hunting me.

I am huge,
Yet soft and gentle.
Stop chasing me, stop hunting me.

I swim through the sea
Hunting my prey.
Stop chasing me, stop hunting me.

I swim around with my pod,
But you catch me in your nets.
Stop chasing me, stop hunting me.

Max Lawes (8) & James Willis (10)
Newton Ferrers CE Primary School, Plymouth

The Gliding Dance Of The Ocean Dolphin

I am the queen of the ocean,
Pale blue and black through silver waters.
Stop chasing me, stop fishing for me.

I am blue through the crashing waves,
Silver through the light of the moon.
Stop chasing me, stop fishing for me.

I glide on through great journeys,
I migrate through tropical seas.
Stop chasing me, stop fishing for me.

I have only a few children.
Why catch them when they're so young?
Stop chasing me, stop fishing for me.

I will live long years
If you will let me.
Stop chasing me, stop fishing for me.

'You are the queen of the ocean,'
A sailor told me one day.
But where are my children?

I am the queen of the ocean,
Black against the cliffs.
Stop chasing me, stop fishing for me.

Georgina McCartney (8), Tom Mears (9) & Bryony Lawes (10)
Newton Ferrers CE Primary School, Plymouth

Shining Angels

Wondrously, a peaceful angel fluttered by.
Drifting with a moonlight sea.
She shimmers in her long floaty dress.
Gracefully her sparkly personality starts to gleam.
Her crystal eyes shine in the moonlight.
Golden hair swooping in the air around her.

Samantha England (10)
Pondhu Primary School, St Austell

Night

Suddenly it began to rain
Suddenly thunder and lightning
Hailstones, like rocks
It made me run to my mum
I cried loudly
I screamed very loudly!
It gave me nightmares
I hid under my bed
I got a torch to see
I stood stump-still
The light shone down.

Anthony Sanders (11)
Pondhu Primary School, St Austell

Faithful Angel

Faithfully, hovering past,
The tranquil angel slid her mysterious hand
Over my cheekbone
Was I touching myself in a mirror?
Feel the angel's silky gown rubbing beside my body.
Angel's hair swings past, the sun beams
Sending shivers up my spine.
Then hovered further into the air.

Sam Loud (10)
Pondhu Primary School, St Austell

Beautiful Angels

Glistening crystal eyes wondering in the moonlight.
Smiles like blossom.
Snowy sunflake dress,
Floating in the golden sunset sky.
Fresh strawberries.
Like a perfume first bought.

Hannah Orchard (10)
Pondhu Primary School, St Austell

The Bright Night's View

The bright night's view is not very new,
The bright night's view, covered in gravel,
The bright night's view, silent and cosy,
The bright night's view, cars slowly strolling over,
The bright night's view.

The bright night's view, covered in bright white lines,
The bright night's view with a thick brick wall,
The bright night's view, a chance to see a gravel covered glance,
The bright night's view, dark and lovely,
The bright night's view.

Amy Littler (10)
Pondhu Primary School, St Austell

Nights Fly By

The shimmering moon dreams silently,
While night flies by, he dreams of dancing stars,
Glamorously shining on the Milky Way,
Like bearers of sunlight guiding the way,
Glittering shooting stars shiver as the clock strikes twelve,
Moon and stars sink down as the sun awakens,
From her warm sleep, to shine through the day.

Daisy Carr (11)
Pondhu Primary School, St Austell

Mysterious Angel

Silently shimmering like stars at night,
She sang so beautifully in the moonlight,
Her wings were as white as snow,
Her golden gown gleaming gracefully,
Her hands were as soft as babies' eyelashes,
I know I won't see her again,
But she'll always be in my heart.

Cavan Boyer (11)
Pondhu Primary School, St Austell

Night

As the sun goes down,
Snails nibble,
And owls venture out hunting,
Owl, fox and dog eye-up their victims,
They dive in for the kill,
Ripping and shredding,
Limb from limb
Trees quiver and hide from these things,
Face to face,
These evil killers cannot be stopped,
Out of the shadows they come,
Will they return,
Tomorrow night?

Breon Wickett (10)
Pondhu Primary School, St Austell

Winter Moon

Glistening stars stare up at the moon,
Blasting their light in the ebony sky,
Wolves howl as if listening to a scary movie,
As the owls swoop high in the dark, misty sky,
The wind screams, as it pushes through,
Through the trees.

As the sky gets dark,
Anxious bunnies scamper into their burrows,
Foxes rush out,
While the moon watches under his heavy lids,
Like a detective searching for clues.

Laura McDonald (10)
Pondhu Primary School, St Austell

Mystery Horse

Misty, silent night,
Moon, shining like there is no tomorrow.
The mystery horse stares at you with his evil eye.
The only noise is an owl, hoot, hoot, hoot.
The mystery horse gallops, jockey on his back,
Whipping him in the races.
While he speeds by.
The moon and stars begin to sing.

Bridie Gabriel (10)
Pondhu Primary School, St Austell

Angels

Dreamily, the angel strikes the little boy's heart
As she wandered into young children's dreams.
Gleaming crystal-blue, innocent eyes
And peeps into the young girl's dream.
Drifts away peacefully into another,
The girl wakes
Crestfallen,
She knows the angel will always be in her heart.

Samuel Rowley (10)
Pondhu Primary School, St Austell

Twilight

At the end of the garden,
Watching the shining sunset.
When the birds are whistling,
When all of the bright lights are about to go on
Peace, the sun, slowly, quietly going down.

Jamie Sanders (11)
Pondhu Primary School, St Austell

Wonderful Angels

Silently, the crystal cloak fell,
Fragile into the silver sparkling moonlight.
Peaceful as a butterfly,
The angel flies
Her dress as white as snow,
Her pretty face glows,
She sings,
Swishing her diamond, delicate dress,
She flies wondrously, wonderfully in the silver sky.

Hayden Thompson (10)
Pondhu Primary School, St Austell

Twilight's Back

At the end of the day,
When the lamps are about to go on,
The dark comes out and twilight's back.

Stars, the black night's zits.
The stars rise up high.
Children, out like a light.
The moon's light is shining.
Stars are shimmering and shining,
Now it is a beautiful night.

William Musgrave (10)
Pondhu Primary School, St Austell

Beautiful Angel

Mysterious, she comes into my eyes.
Beautiful, looking after me.
A beautiful angel.
A silky white dress.
A smell of blooming blossoms.
She never sleeps at all.

Chad Busby (11)
Pondhu Primary School, St Austell

Young Writers - Little Laureates Poems From Devon & Cornwall

Forgiving Angel

Magical luminous moonlight,
Glistening softly,
On glamorous angel's gleaming wings,
Smoothly, sweet smells,
Perfume from Heaven's angel,
Golden locks swaying around
Forgiving crystal-blue eyes,
Cherry-red lips,
Angels in Heaven;
Angels in my dreams.

Keyna Summers (11)
Pondhu Primary School, St Austell

Mysterious Angel

Mysteriously, highlighted against the peaceful rising sun,
Gracefully picking her way through harmonious moonlight,
Shimmering dress billowing in the evening breeze.

Her skin, as clear as crystals, singing sweetly,
Yet sadly in the gleaming mist, drifting aimlessly,
Her wings, soft as rose petals, swishing joyously in lonely heavens.

Nicole Gilbert (10)
Pondhu Primary School, St Austell

Amazing Angels

Wondrously, gracefully, floating by,
Angels drifted like dandelion seeds, every golden glimmer,
Sparkle, shimmer,
Was all delightful and deluxe.
Every movement, every step, seemed to be
Rehearsed for hundreds of years.

Thomas Tyrrell (10)
Pondhu Primary School, St Austell

Angel

Tiny angel always in my dreams,
Just like a soulmate,
Shares all her things,
This little angel has a wonderful name,
Her name is Angelina,
A kind and helpful angel,
She always thinks of me,
Angelina always in my heart,
Will be with you and me forever,
Tiny angel always in my dreams.

Shannon Caulfield (10)
Pondhu Primary School, St Austell

Twilight

The gleaming stars drift upon the atmosphere,
Beams of amazing amber sun,
Zooming down, a racing car taking first place,
Bright moon swishing around the pitch-black sky,
Owls flying around the sizzling moon,
Feathers swishing along the atmosphere,
Owls' eyes shining as street lights,
Baby owls waiting to be fed,
Owls flying down to get their victims to feed the baby owls.

Hannah Noy (11)
Pondhu Primary School, St Austell

Angels

Beautiful angel, she danced like a thousand diamonds,
To prove love is real,
She swishes her wings, in the sunlight.

Chad Ackrell (10)
Pondhu Primary School, St Austell

Angel Breeze

Sparkling personality,
Gliding in the soft wind,
Forgiving, wondrous blue eyes,
Glistening smile.

Generous lightened heart,
As soft as a baby's cheek,
Unrecognisable face in the dark,
An angel, never rests.
Always by your side.

Jade Truman (10)
Pondhu Primary School, St Austell

Hail Horses

Hail bouncing off rooftops,
Like a horse's hooves on the ground,
Prancing with its foal,
Playing around,
Sun on their backs,
Hail melts like sweat,
Running off into the sparkling rivers.

Emma Rowe (9)
St Buryan Primary School, Penzance

Snow Bunnies

The snow dances in the sky,
And floats down like fluffy bunnies,
It hops across the icy floor,
And skips into a field,
It dives into a burrow,
Then goes to sleep
On a soft blanket.

Olivia Barnes (9)
St Buryan Primary School, Penzance

Windy Whales

The wind
Flops and dances
Like whales
Kicking and flicking
Their tails in the sky
With waves of cloud.
The wind blows trees
Wild and free
As whales in the sea.

Ana Young (9)
St Buryan Primary School, Penzance

Lightning

Lightning sneaking silently
Ready to pounce
Heavy breathing, creeping
Closer, closer . . .
Bang!
The lightning strikes
People yelping,
Yelping.

Luke Piggott (10)
St Buryan Primary School, Penzance

The Wind

The wind came
As a horse
With its tail flowing
Behind it.
Its echoing neigh,
Howling into the distance.
Its thundering hooves
Slowly drifting away.

Justine Nixon (10)
St Buryan Primary School, Penzance

My Visit To London

We're on the train and off we go,
Skies of cloud filled with snow.

It looks very cold outside,
As we pass the crashing tide.

As we see a dashing fox,
It's like we're travelling in a box.

Passing through lots of stops,
People playing with spinning tops.

When we see the London Eye,
We all think, *now isn't that high!*

Laughing, cheering, giggling,
That's what I like to be hearing.

We're all happy and excited,
And we're all pleased and delighted.

I go on the London Underground,
You can hear the rhythm of the sound.

Now I feel extremely sleepy,
I also feel a bit weepy.

Kellie Williams (9)
St Buryan Primary School, Penzance

Wind

The wind howls,
Like a captured dog searching for freedom.
Tearing at trees,
Hurling itself against glass windows.
Leaping high up to go down the chimney,
Rushing through the swing in the garden
Then bounding over the hedge,
Around the hills and woods,
To blow at the mountains far, far away.

Tegen Butterfield (10)
St Buryan Primary School, Penzance

The Lightning Storm

Thunder growls like a tiger
Trying to get to sleep.
It roars so loud it echoes
Around the city streets
Petrifying everything
And people in their houses.

Lightning is the claws
Of a tiger sitting on its haunches,
Getting ready to pounce,
It waits
. . . then suddenly it stuns its prey
With its razor-sharp claws,
Then scatters off.

Jakob Fox (10)
St Buryan Primary School, Penzance

Hailstones

Millions of cats
Pouncing away

Some heading for shelter
Others catching their prey

Cats scratching
Pouncing at the window

Yet when the sun
Comes up
Scatter in
All directions again.

Laura Sutton (10)
St Buryan Primary School, Penzance

First Adventure

I walked up a very high hill,
I saw a fish that had a gill.

I went to the warm sunny beach,
I ate a nice juicy peach.

I played in the cold foaming waves,
Where the grey-black basking shark bathes.

Now it's really truly done,
It was very, very fun.

I got so very, very cold,
And this is the story that I told!

Abbey Thomas (9)
St Buryan Primary School, Penzance

The Sun

The sun comes up
Like a peacock's tail
Rising upon the clouds
Gleaming over the mountains
And shining down the stream.
The sun puts on his hat,
The sun puts on his shades,
Smiling at the children
Down at the small beach.
The sun takes off his hat,
The sun takes off his shades
Ready for next time,
So he can come and play.

Shannon Harris (10)
St Buryan Primary School, Penzance

London Trip

Hurry Mum, we're going to be late,
Quick, quick they're shutting the gate

At the moment we're on the train,
Why do we go through the rain?

There's a white horse carved in the hill,
I hope nobody gets very ill

It takes five hours from here to there,
Where are we? Oh where? Oh where?

We stop at Paddington where it is dirty,
All the people there are very shirty.

In London it's very smoky,
Be careful now or you'll be choky

We're in the park, we can see lots of geese,
It really is a masterpiece

There's a squirrel it's very pretty,
I do not know if they are witty

The underground is very hot,
There's lots of people, lots and lots

There's the London Eye, it's really tall,
Hold on tight or you'll fall

Buckingham Palace is very large,
There's two men outside, they call them guards

We pass a statue, I think it is the queen,
It is Victoria she looks very mean

We're on the boat cruising down,
My seat is coloured a light brown

Now we're going back home,
Here we go with a great big moan.

Imogen Forster (9)
St Buryan Primary School, Penzance

Hurricane Madness

Hurricane spinning around
Like a Tasmanian devil
Destroying everything in its sight,
Picking up trees and houses
Making the sky black
The sea popping up and down
And boats sinking.
The Tasmanian devil is very happy
Destroying his prey.
His footsteps are like hammers banging wood.

James Margerison (10)
St Buryan Primary School, Penzance

The Way To London

White horse hill rushes past
As do mobile phone masts.
Over an iron bridge we fly,
If we had wings we would be in the sky.
Passing fields full of cows,
Farmers working hard with ploughs.

Haydn Tremethick (10)
St Buryan Primary School, Penzance

The Wolf's Sharp Jaw

Wind howls like a wolf
Wind howls over the pier
Watching you
The wind swoops down
And catches you
Like a wolf's sharp jaw.

Charlotte Trembath (9)
St Buryan Primary School, Penzance

The Fog

The fog comes,
On old autumn leaves,
Slowly creeping into the city.

She stops,
She stares,
At the silence standing before her
And hears the silence beating
Like a drum . . .

Fog stands silent, lonely as a jaguar.

Caitlin Eley (10)
St Buryan Primary School, Penzance

The Thunder And Lightning

The thunder roars
Resembling
A mad tiger,
Its roaring a warning
Vicious snakes
Fight with the angry tiger,
Lighting up the sky.

Teigan Delbridge (9)
St Buryan Primary School, Penzance

The Sand Storm

The sand storm is a snake
Slithering for its prey
When it strikes it's caught its prey
One big bite
And the snake is strong.

Tom Price (9)
St Buryan Primary School, Penzance

Flight

We started to move, it was very slow,
We knew there were hundreds of miles to go

Through Switzerland, Italy and France
Looking at fluffy clouds, wanting to dance

Over the Alps covered in snow
The people know there's not long to go!

Flying down ready to land
Staring at the golden sands.

Cameron Ness (10)
St Buryan Primary School, Penzance

Lightning

I see a flashing snake
He's looking for his prey
I see the snake up in the clouds
With another snake
Their forked tongues
Taste the air
Waiting for their prey.

Jacob Cowell (9)
St Buryan Primary School, Penzance

Dancing Girls

The cloud giving birth to snow
Dancing gracefully
As a girl in the night
With the full moon,
The sun comes up
And the girls turn to their beds,
Very slowly the sun melts
The little sleeping girls.

Bethany Mason (10)
St Buryan Primary School, Penzance

The Ferry

We're on the ferry in the sea,
Hours it seems, no only three
The ferry makes a lot of noise
In a bag I've brought some toys
On the deck it is very wet
We spy a fishing boat dragging a net
The trails from the ship stretch on for miles
All the way to the Scilly Isles
In our cabin it's pretty warm
Luckily there's not a storm
Finally at France we arrive
Now to start the five hour drive.

Ross Thomas (10)
St Buryan Primary School, Penzance

Autumn

Swishing leaves swooping down to the floor
Getting huffed and puffed out of the tree
Dark brown to tropical yellow
Like a hawk being shot out of the tree
And you can see them glide.
Brightening the ground, shaped into a crispy blanket
With a muddy smell
Autumn grabs his hat
Ready to fly away
Autumn is an owl
Watching day and night
Until one morning it will go to sleep,
No more flights
Fewer flowers fly across the sky,
Less and less every day.
Getting colder every day
Will it ever return?

Patryk Rudnik (11) & Oliver Cornell (10)
St Day & Caharrack Community School, Redruth

Autumn

The autumn bride was dressed in gold and stood upon the hill,
Her skin was white, her eyes were bright and her gown was made
With skill.
Her blusterous veil blew over the land,
There were Michaelmas daisies clutched in her hand,
And the crimson sun, that was setting fast, awed at her beauty as
it passed.
The trees scattered their confetti, maroon, ochre and red,
Swirling and twirling round her bonny ginger head.
Great oaks bent as her auburn altar,
A chestnut case was her emerald ring,
As her communion the bare trees stood with her,
And for the choir, the birds did sing.

But no great groom stood waiting at the altar,
Onto her finger no one slipped her emerald ring,
And weeping like a willow, she slipped away to winter,
Slipped away to winter and slipped into the spring . . .

Holly Summerson (10)
St Day & Caharrack Community School, Redruth

Autumn

Autumn comes just once a year,
Soon before the Christmas cheer.
Leaves float down from naked trees,
Tumbling between the bumblebees.

Squirrels search and scratch around,
Taking leaves upon the ground.
Animals hibernate in their beds,
All coloured leaves yellow, gold and red.

Holly Truman (10)
St Day & Caharrack Community School, Redruth

Autumn

Autumn is a wizard,
Casting spells on trees,
Making the leaves flutter down,

Crackling and crunching leaves,
Drifting off the trees,
Beautiful colours all red, brown and orange,
Like butterflies fluttering down.

Prickly conkers all spiky and spiny,
Like hedgehogs shuffling about.

Stiff acorns dangling from a tree,
Occasionally falling,
Down to the ground
Like bombs blowing up a city full of leaves!

Ella Jarvis (10)
St Day & Caharrack Community School, Redruth

Autumn

Autumn is a butterfly
With its wings of golden-brown, hot orange and fire red,
Fluttering down off treetops
Stuttering across the ground,
Making a crackling, crunching, crispy sound,
Like a band that only has a few notes to play!

Katie Jones (11)
St Day & Caharrack Community School, Redruth

Autumn

Autumn is a pot of paint,
Spreading its autumn powers,
Turning crispy leaves autumn colours,
Golden brown, burning-red,
Like fewer flowers,
Wind is lifting,
Acorns acting,
Birds are moving, migrating,
Soaring, flying across the blue,
Out with the old and in with the new,
Days getting shorter,
Also very cold,
Very, very breezy,
People getting sneezy.

Tamara Orchard (10)
St Day & Caharrack Community School, Redruth

Autumn

The autumn is a child climbing
Trees and knocking leaves
That crunch under my feet,
Climbing up, up, up spreading colour
Of gold, red, yellow, brown,
Just like butterflies swooping down in the breeze,
Squirrels flitting all around trying
To find their berries that they've
Hidden down and down
Underneath their cherries,
There's nothing like an orange field
Full of leaves and empty trees.

Chloe Roberts (10)
St Day & Caharrack Community School, Redruth

Autumn

Autumn arrived fairly late,
Leaving leaves by the gate,
Knocked upon my front door,
After decorating the muddy moor,
He asked to see our garden green,
Where we had presently been,
No leaves on the grass,
All upon our tree,
Then old Mr Autumn asked us to leave him be,
When he left,
The leaves were gone and autumn went via the front door
We heard the crunch beneath his boot,
And summer had gone.

Isabella Cochrane (10)
St Day & Caharrack Community School, Redruth

Autumn

Autumn swooped to the floor,
Leaving leaves all over.
Blowing the leaves off all the small trees.
Brown, orange, red and yellow, all the colours of the leaves
Autumn is a murderer
Killing all the flowers.
Fluttering flowers float by
Oh sorry that's in the summer
Because all the flowers are dead.

Joe Goldsworthy (9)
St Day & Caharrack Community School, Redruth

Autumn!

Autumn is a sweet that's colourful!
Autumn is like a burning piece of gold shining brightly,
As she drops her golden leaves and runs through the forest,
As she runs the sun burns,
She settles down to sleep as winter takes her place,
Autumn does not mind that winter has taken her place.

Katie Fletcher (9)
St Day & Caharrack Community School, Redruth

Autumn

Autumn was walking on the crunchy leaves
Running through them.
Brown and orange,
Cold, cold, cold, like the North Pole.
Fleecy wool coats to keep out the cold.

Chloe Dingle (10)
St Day & Caharrack Community School, Redruth

Autumn

Autumn is a silver butterfly
Floating around in the sky
Like a leaf falling down from the bare trees
Days getting colder, dress up warm
Crunchy leaves on the floor moving about
Orangey and already falling down like floaty flowers fluttering down.

Jasmine Bennetts (9)
St Day & Caharrack Community School, Redruth

Yippee - Cinquains

Yippee!
It is today
We are going away
We're going on a plane to Spain
Yippee!

Yippee!
We have arrived
Watch out Spain, I am here!
We are staying in a villa
Yippee!

Yippee!
Learning Spanish
I love the gorgeous food
The temperature is quite hot
Yippee!

Yippee!
I love the beach
Never want to leave here
It is time to go home, oh no!
Oh no!

Charlotte Rogers (10)
St John's RC Primary School, Tiverton

The Park - Cinquains

The park
The park is fun
There are swings and seesaws
Lots of people go to the park
It's great!

The swings
The swings are fun
Young children go on them
Lots of people go to the park
Swinging!

The pool
Water splashing
Children laugh and have fun
Lots of people go to the park
Splash! Splash!

People
People have fun
People eat their picnics
Lots of people go to the park
Chatting!

Jordan Haskings (10)
St John's RC Primary School, Tiverton

The War

There was a world war
People were dragged in, others saw
There was a lot more.

Lots of people died
The advantage was to hide
People couldn't decide.

It was a big battle
The guns began to rattle
It was at a settle.

It was in Japan
Most of the Japanese ran
A lot of them swam.

Injuries to mend
The war drove us round the bend
It's come to an end.

Toby Hogan (10)
St John's RC Primary School, Tiverton

War!

Bang! As an airship flew overhead,
Then I got woken up out of my own bed,
The sergeant called me as he helped me up,
So I marched into battle and heard a big rattle,
The guns were loaded, an atomic bomb exploded
Some Germans were dead but most of them fled,
We won, the Germans were gone.

Alex Wright (10)
St John's RC Primary School, Tiverton

Young Writers - Little Laureates Poems From Devon & Cornwall

Hallowe'en

Hallowe'en night, Hallowe'en night
Shall I tell you how it started?
Hallowe'en night, Hallowe'en night
On Hallowe'en night all the ghouls and ghosts
Came down to Earth
Hallowe'en night, Hallowe'en night
The people wanted a solution
Hallowe'en night, Hallowe'en night
So a farmer got a pumpkin
Hallowe'en night, Hallowe'en night
And into it he carved a scary face
Hallowe'en night, Hallowe'en night
And into it he placed a candle
Hallowe'en night, Hallowe'en night
To give it an eerie glow
To keep the ghouls away tonight
Hallowe'en night, Hallowe'en night.

Daniel Martin (10)
Trannack CP School, Helston

Sun And The Sea The Future Set In London

The sun shines through the window like stabbing swords.
The sea is clear like a clear diamond.
The sea will never end and never bend.
The sea crashes to the sand.
The sun burns like a flaming hot fire.
The sea is an emerald gem.
The sea is rough and it crashes on the harbour wall.
Coming more closer and closer then it swept away.

Tattianna Haslam (9)
Trannack CP School, Helston

I Have To Go To School Today

I have to go to school today
As bad as it is I have to go
Like hail as it has to snow
It's cold and boring and I get sleepy
It makes me hyper and very bleepy
My friends are funny and very bright
But I'm the one who gets a fight
I support Liverpool but my friends support Man U
But they suck and smell as bad as an old rotten shoe
It's time for maths it's really fun
It's like being in a sea heated by the sun
But it's not it's so sad
It makes me really, really mad
It's time for literacy it's not very fun
It's Mr Harpin now, he's definitely going to run
His eyes are pins and his ears are like a hawk
Now he's writing with some chalk
It's finally the end of the day, yes I'm happy, hip hip hooray.

Alex Atkinson-Sims (10)
Trannack CP School, Helston

Ten Things In Santa's Sack

Chomped carrot that Rudolf has just eaten
Half-eaten mince pie that Santa has eaten on his travels

Pack of pens that Santa forgot to deliver
A stuffed teddy that Santa cuddles

Wrapping paper for wrapping presents
Ribbon to wrap around the sleigh

Sticker book for children
Plastic horse for girls
And a pair of red shoes to play the Wizard of Oz
Barbie bag for holding your swim kit.

Elleanor Atkinson-Sims (9)
Trannack CP School, Helston

Young Writers - Little Laureates Poems From Devon & Cornwall

The Moll Troll

The Moll troll lives under a bridge,
He has warts all over his face,
And he looks like a dead rat.
He smells like a rotten bowl of stew,
And is as fast as a cheetah,
He's as grumpy as a grampa and eats like a dog
He lives in a mud pool and thinks he's very cool
His skin is green
And his eyes are red
His feet look like balls of rocks
And his toenails look like slugs
He is the most
Horrible
Troll in the
World.

Alfie Pulley (9)
Trannack CP School, Helston

The Monster

It is strong and vicious
Its teeth are razor-sharp
Its body is like a wiggling worm
Nails like metal teeth
It looks like a hairy tarantula.
Has a tail like a shooting laser
It moves like a steel tank.
I know you don't believe me
That a monster is coming closer, Mum.
But it's getting closer!

Arghhhhhhhhhhh!

James Willcock (9)
Trannack CP School, Helston

Hallowe'en Poem

Hallowe'en night, Hallowe'en night.
Is coming around the town.
People are scared, people are dressed up
The moon is out and the stars are twinkling
Some children are getting candy
From mums and dads
There are witches, wolves, ghosts and skeletons everywhere
Hallowe'en night, Hallowe'en night
Dark and spooky
Ooooh!

Bethan Lewis (10)
Trannack CP School, Helston

Horses

H air of brown, white and black
O ver the hills
R unning fast
S kidding fast
E ating slow
S wishing its tail.

Amy Rossiter (8)
Trannack CP School, Helston

The Night Sky

The stars are bright
And so is the night.
The moon is like
A glowing sphere
In the sky.
Shimmering, like the moon can fly.
Into the bright night sky.

Georgia Slater (10)
Trannack CP School, Helston

The Dragon

In the field
You might like to bathe
Not in this field
There's a
Dragon!
The dragon looks like
A big red bird, he has red eyes,
Long claws, long horns and hot fire!
Once you go down to the field
Promise me you will look out
For the dragon, he will go
Roar!

Bradley Broughton (8)
Trannack CP School, Helston

My Little Brother

My little brother is as cute as a puppy

As funny as a clown and

I love him so much

His eyes are as greeny-blue as the sea
And I love him so much

He is as silly as a monkey
And he makes me laugh
And I love him so much

When he talks he sounds like a kitten going miaow, miaow
And I love him so much.

Daniella Atkinson (10)
Trannack CP School, Helston

The Sea

The sea is like a prowling cat
A whirlwind of blue
The sea is like a pool of glass
A clear blue diamond
The sea is like the eye of a blue whale
A flowerbed of blue
Shiny blue plastic against the sun
Do you like the sea too?

Alice Ockwell (9)
Trannack CP School, Helston

Rose

A rose is like a shiny red ruby
Its petals are like flaky cloth
Its prickles are like rusty spines
Its leaves are like emerald diamonds
Its stalk is like a frozen snake
A rose is like warm flowing blood
It's different from any other flower.

It's special . . .

Cora Lappel (10)
Trannack CP School, Helston

Horses

Horses are black, brown and white
They can gallop as fast as the wind
Over the hill and away they go
Galloping horses
They are Fallabella, Arab, Shetland too
Shire, Haflinger, Dartmoor too
And Welsh section A, B, C and D
Horses are truly the best animal you can see!

Megan Williams (8)
Trannack CP School, Helston

The Wind

I blow through the trees
I make the grass sway
I even make some trees blow away
I'm as fast as light
Put your coat on, it's cold tonight.
Does anyone know what I am?
I am the wind that blows day and night
Hip hip hooray
The wind today
Hip hip hooray
The wind today, today, today.

Amy Martin (8)
Trannack CP School, Helston

Autumn

In autumn time leaves turn gold
Like a bucket of sand.
The trees are like trunks with massive splinters.
The brambles are full of big fat juicy blackberries
The green grass is gone the brown is here
Plants are dead but winter is coming
So let's party.

Caleb Martins (10)
Trannack CP School, Helston

Bonfire Night

The sound of fireworks, going bang and pop.
Everyone yelling, shouting.
Everyone enjoying the fireworks.
Come out! Come out! Come out and play.
Come out with us on Bonfire Night.

Leanne Baguley (8)
Wendron CE Primary School, Helston

Bonfire Night

It's Bonfire Night, everybody's there.
Everybody goes, 'Ooh, ahh!'
Whoosh, bang!
There are children running,
Babies are crying, I've got a headache.
Oh it's Bonfire Night, it's the best day of the year.
Oh no it's stopped
We're going home now
Not to worry, we'll be back next year.

Katie-Jo Tomlinson (8)
Wendron CE Primary School, Helston

Bonfire Night

I heard the cracklers, fizz and pop
I won't be goin' too soon,
I heard my little sister cry,
As that old rocket went.

The ones I call da 'fizzlers'
Just went outa' control,
I heard it pop, then we stopped,
Then the crowd started whoopin'.

Tamzin Reynolds (9)
Wendron CE Primary School, Helston

Mr Bat

Once there was a good bat,
Who liked a green big mat.
He saw a big fat rat,
Who was on his big mat.
He bit the big fat rat,
Then sat back on his big mat.

Harry Phipps (7)
Wendron CE Primary School, Helston

Bonfire Night

B ang! the fireworks go
O ver there is a whoosh.
N oises whizz, pop and crackle.
F ireworks crackle, whizz, boom.
I nventing cakes and fireworks.
R abbits hopping in their holes.
E ggs and bacon for tea.
 I love Bonfire Night
 It is brilliant.

Avena Makin (9)
Wendron CE Primary School, Helston

The Night Of The Bang!

The fire crackling
Popping and banging,
Fireworks squealing
Whizzing, banging
A multicoloured rainbow,
Babies crying, screaming, crying.
People sighing, cheering, bang!
Goes the fire all the time,
Everyone loves Bonfire Night.

Ronan Fraser (9)
Wendron CE Primary School, Helston

The Dog

Once there was a dog
Who went for a jog.
He fell in a bog.
And held onto a log
He got lost in the fog
And never finished his jog!

Jack Williams (7)
Wendron CE Primary School, Helston

Fireworks And Bonfires

Every night when it is Bonfire Night they go bang and when it is
fireworks night they go pop.

And when the fireworks are lit, the bonfire is on lots and lots of people
stand outside and watch them go.

When all the people watch it some people eat popcorn and some
people eat baked potatoes with cheese on.

And the oldest person in your family has to light it.
No little people can light it, only when they are adults.

Kristin Fern (8)
Wendron CE Primary School, Helston

My Dog

My dog is a rough collie like Lassie,
Her name is Thistle but she is not prickly at all,
She is a big, soft, fluffy, hairy ball.
We take her for long walks on the beach,
And she rounds us up like sheep.
We chase each other around the garden and fall rolling in a heap.
She wags her tail when she sees me, I give her a pat and a treat.
Me and my dog Thistle, the best dog I'll ever meet.

Jack Rhodes (7)
Wendron CE Primary School, Helston

Bonfire Night

It is Bonfire Night, everyone is shouting.
Everyone is watching the beautiful fireworks
It sounds like this bang and whoosh.
The colours of the fireworks red, yellow, blue and green.
The sound of the fire is pop, crackle, squeal.

Sophie Bromfield (8)
Wendron CE Primary School, Helston

Bonfire Night

On Bonfire Night the fireworks crackle,
Everyone there is in a big hassle.
On Bonfire Night.

On Bonfire Night the rockets fly,
The fire crackles, whooshes and crackles
On Bonfire Night.

On Bonfire Night all the children squeal with delight
On Bonfire Night.

Katie Humphries (8)
Wendron CE Primary School, Helston

Bonfire Night

On Bonfire Night you hear lots of bangs, crackles, whooshes
And lots of pops and squeals.
Ooh, ahh, eee, ooh.
You could hear lots of people sighing and chatting on Bonfire Night.

Sparklers make bright light.
The fire crackles and is very hot and bright.

Andrew Coulston (9)
Wendron CE Primary School, Helston

Bonfire Night

On Bonfire Night the fire crackles,
On Bonfire Night, fireworks fizz, pop and bang,
On Bonfire Night you can hear people's feet on the cold hard ground,
On Bonfire Night screaming, squealing fireworks whizz through
$$\text{The night.}$$

Chloe Crimmen (8)
Wendron CE Primary School, Helston

Bonfire Night

On Bonfire Night when the Catherine wheels whizz,
The children's sparklers start to fizz,
The fireworks, such a pretty sight,
All go off on Bonfire Night.

When all the fireworks all start booming,
All the people start oohing,
The fireworks give some people a fright,
All go off on Bonfire Night.

The fireworks all make a bang,
The little children thought they sang,
But actually it was a squeal,
The children love the Catherine wheel,
The fireworks make it so alight,
All go off on Bonfire Night.

Diani Laity (9)
Wendron CE Primary School, Helston

The World

The world is very precious
It is here for you and me
We should all take care of it
For everyone to see.

It won't be here forever
But while it is we know
We should Reduce, Reuse, Recycle
So we can let the planet grow.

Brooke Fraser (8)
Wendron CE Primary School, Helston

Bonfire Night

B urning and crackling of the flames.
O ohing and ahhing people.
N ight falling so quickly.
F ireworks fizzing and whizzing everywhere.
I t gets so hot when you go near the bonfire.
R iding fast to get there in your car.
E erie sounds in the sky.

N oises of clanging and banging of fireworks.
I ce-cold sausages from the shop on the barbeque stand.
G uy Fawkes burning wildly, quickly
H eating up everywhere and big pop here and there.
T alking and chatting everywhere.

Lydia Curnow (9)
Wendron CE Primary School, Helston

Bonfire Night

Fireworks popping
Ashes dropping
As the fireworks go *bang! Bang!*

Fire is crackling
People are sighing
As the fireworks go *bang! Bang!*

Fireworks are squealing
Fireworks are whizzing
As the fireworks go *bang!*

Cameron Hinton Rowe (9)
Wendron CE Primary School, Helston

Bonfire Night

B ang, *whoosh, crackle*. That's what I hear.
O n and on all night long!
N ever stop, *crack, crack, pop!*
F ireworks, fireworks, go bang!
I hear a whoosh, bang, whizzing sound.
R ound, round, the Catherine wheel goes.
E very Bonfire Night, fireworks!

N owadays pretty lights! Ooh, argh.
I 'll stand here waiting all night long.
G rowing up, higher and higher.
H it the sky, do the fireworks
T onight is Bonfire Night!

Chloe Taylor (8)
Wendron CE Primary School, Helston

Big Balloon

Silence is like a light brown labyrinth,
Fear is like black and red blood,
Anger is green like the unfortunate aliens,
Laughter is red like polka dots on a big balloon,
The heat is orange like a dragon's flames.

Tom Bennett (10)
Wendron CE Primary School, Helston

Bonfire Night

Bang! as the people go, 'Ooh!'
The night of Bonfire Night.
'Ahhh!' as the rocket goes *roar*.
Angry rockets making terrible noises.
The beautiful glazes that the fireworks make.

Rebecca Care (8)
Wendron CE Primary School, Helston

Young Writers - Little Laureates Poems From Devon & Cornwall

Bonfire Night

B onfires are very fun,
O n bonfires there's lots of smoke;
N o one can see through all the smoke.
F unny fireworks flying in the sky.
I love fireworks dashing in the sky
R ockets make me scared before fireworks,
E veryone is shocked when they hear them.

Bonfire Night.

N o one can see through all the smoke,
I love fireworks dashing in the sky.
G o outside and see the good fireworks,
H ear the bonfire flames crackling in the air,
T o and fro it goes with the rockets.

Pollyanna Webb (8)
Wendron CE Primary School, Helston

The Night Of Wonders

Oh yes, yes it's Bonfire Night,
A night filled with surprise and delight.

Fireworks *booming* here and there,
Even louder than a bear!

Pink and purple and green and white,
All fill the sky on Bonfire Night.

'Ohh' and *'Ahh'* fill the night,
Huge explosions of bright light!

It's nearly here the big finale,
Then we can go in and have a party!

The fireworks are done,
Everyone has gone.

All the sparklers disappear,
Fun again next year!

Milly Hayton (9)
Wendron CE Primary School, Helston

Bonfire Night

The sound of fireworks just about to come up,
The fire sizzling,
And the whoosh of the fireworks
Also of the wood of the crackling
And the sigh when it floats down

Fireworks whizzing and sizzling,
All of the fireworks end with a *bang!*
People chatting, babies crying all scared of the pop.

Isabella Corbridge (9)
Wendron CE Primary School, Helston

A Bonfire Poem

The fireworks so noisy fill the sky,
Bang! Crackle! Pop!
The fire so smoky,
Makes the adults cry,
Bang! Crackle! Pop!
The sparklers so bright,
Shine like torchlight,
Bang! Crackle! Pop!
Watch out Dad,
The firework is going off!

Alex Hayton (9)
Wendron CE Primary School, Helston

Cheeky Words

Laughter is orange like bubblegum,
Anger is red like a dragon's flames
Happiness is pink like ice cream,
Fun is mint-green like sweets,
Sadness is blue like sea,
Hate is grey like mist.

Terri Baguley (9)
Wendron CE Primary School, Helston

Senses And Colours

Anger is red like bright red blood,
Love is like hot-pink bubblegum,
Hunger is yellow like a ferocious lion,
Fear is grey like a pit of wet darkness,
Hate is red like the red sky in the morning,
Sadness is green like wet grass when it's been raining,
Happiness is like indigo when people's faces light up
When they open Christmas presents.
Silence is silver like a shadow on the ground.

Lowena Mudge (10)
Wendron CE Primary School, Helston

Plain White

Fear is black like a black hole,
Anger is white like an exploding gun,
Darkness is dark blue like a rough sea,
Sadness is grey like a broken heart,
Hate is purple like the tips of mountains,
Hunger is brown like hamburgers.
Silence is cream like cream marshmallows.

Daniel Ferrie (9)
Wendron CE Primary School, Helston

My Feelings

Fear is black like the solar system,
Happiness is turquoise like the blue, blue sea,
Anger is volcano orange like a blazing fire,
Fun is pink like a bright rose,
Sadness is grey like a droopy thunder cloud.
Love is dark red like a juicy plum, just right!
Silence is blue like a silvery mist.

Cherie Watters (9)
Wendron CE Primary School, Helston

Happy Colours

Happiness is golden like gold coins,
Joys is yellow like the seaside sand,
Fun is black and white like a football,
Hunger is green like pure sick,
Laughter is black for I have never laughed,
Silence is white like the clouds,
Hate is fiery purple like a snake's slitted eyes,
Fear is clear like watery eyes,
Love is red like the human blood,
Anger is orange like man-made fire,
Darkness is black like death.

Sam Eyres (10)
Wendron CE Primary School, Helston

Emotions

Silence is cream like soft marshmallows,
Hate is black like a whirlwind of darkness,
Fun is pink like bubbles,
Hunger is brown like an ox roast,
Anger is red like blood.

Fear is green bomb shells,
Love is crimson like lips,
Darkness is grey like Hell,
Happiness is blue like the sky,
Sadness is purple like rubbish
Laughter is yellow like boiled swede.

Jacob Webb (10)
Wendron CE Primary School, Helston

Coloured Emotions

Laughter is pink like bubbles
Laughter is red like a rose
Darkness is black like space
Darkness is navy like the bottom of the ocean
Fun is orange like the beaming sun
Fun is yellow like the smiling sun
Sadness is black like death
Sadness is grey and white like a cold winter's evening
Happiness is purple like cold ice cream
Happiness is aqua like a sea of whipped cream
Hunger is green like seaweed
Hunger is green like sick
Love is white like a cloud of candyfloss
Love is hot-pink like squashy marshmallows
Love is as red as a lollipop.

Brittany Laity (11)
Wendron CE Primary School, Helston

Hearing Is Immense

When the sky turns dark, silence descends
The words of the owl are wise
The song of the cricket is heart-breaking
The echo of the wood pigeon is breathless.
When the sky turns light noise peers around us,
The bird's melody is exquisite,
The butterfly's wings tell a story
As the joy of hearing is immense.

Emily Rhodes (10)
Wendron CE Primary School, Helston

Describing Colours

Laughter is spring-green, like the whispering trees,
Fun is orange, like a bouncing ball,
Happiness is bright yellow, like the gleaming sun,
Ambition is dark violet, like sunset clouds.

Sadness is grey, like a pit,
Anger is red, like fiery flames,
Fear is brown, like a bear,
Darkness is black, like a black hole,
Hate is luminous green, like jealousy,
Hunger is dark red, like blood.

Isobel Fern (11)
Wendron CE Primary School, Helston

Colour Crazy

Fun is pink like happiness.
Hunger is white like misty skies.
Happiness is orange like the beaming sun.
Hate is black like coffins.
Silence is brown like the dusty roads.
Sadness is blue like the cold snow.
Fear is red like juicy tomatoes.
Anger is yellow like a flashing light.
Darkness is black like nothing.

Verity Bray (10)
Wendron CE Primary School, Helston

Autumn

Children dressing up warm,
Ready to go for a walk.

Damp green grass,
Wet from the morning dew.

Tall silent trees,
Watching the children go by.

The cold still lake,
Awaits its next victim.

The cawing crows fly by,
Heading for their nests.

The children go home,
To have hot chocolate by the fire.

Heather MacNeil (10)
Wendron CE Primary School, Helston

Rainbow Madness

Hunger is brown like a beefburger.
Hate is black like black Airwave gum.
Fear is purple like purple faces.
Anger is blue like the sea tossing a ship around.
Darkness is black like a piece of coal.
Fun is yellow as the sun giggles.
Love is red like red roses.
Laughter is pink as my smile is pink.
Silence is green like the whispers of trees.
Sadness is grey like the mist of the rooftops.

Jessica Goodchild (10)
Wendron CE Primary School, Helston

Dreams

Pink magical cats
Swaying in the
Wild wind
Mystical waters
Madly splashing
In rattling rain
Furious flames
Dancing happily
In the
Shining moonlight
Boisterous rain
Swimming
Gracefully in
Snowy stars
Stormy sand
Scattering in
Furious mad
Moons
Snowy snowflakes
Carefully drifting
Down to the
Happily singing
Ground!
Dreams!

Amy Nassaris (8) & Emma Moore (7)
Yealmpstone Farm Primary School

Dreams

In the dark night twinkling stars appear while dreams come true.
When the moon pops up they all start to play
But when it's morning dreams go away.

Emily Williams (8)
Yealmpstone Farm Primary School

War Time

Don't know where I am
Know I shouldn't be here
But can you hear that?
Don't know what it is
Running . . . Why
Are they running?
Wish I knew what to do
I was very anxious
About this then I could
See a big black plane
Sky filled with dark mist
Someone captured me
And said, 'It's an air raid
Get in the shelter!'
In the shelter I heard a bomb
It hit the shelter with a crash
I closed my eyes and counted to ten
Wishing I would walk up knowing
That was a dream
I woke up huffing and puffing
I'm glad I'm home in my soft warm big comfy bed.

Tia Auguste (8)
Yealmpstone Farm Primary School

Dreams

Dreams are for sleeping
Dreams are for daydreaming
You can have dreams that will work anytime
Dreams are happy, they can cheer you up, especially slow dreams.
Dreams are in your bedroom, in your head full of joy
You could eat a whole bowl of ice cream, yum, yum!
You could do anything in your dreams.

Ellen Granville (7)
Yealmpstone Farm Primary School

Dreams, Dreams, Animal Dreams

Your dream is like a searchlight
Shimmering and shining in the sky
Slowly
Your dream is like a German bomb
Running
Through the sky quickly.
Your dream has you in a gas mask
Sitting
In an air-raid shelter
Crying madly

Your dream has a bunny sitting quietly
Your dream has you twisting,
Twirling,
Curly, whirly.

Round and round.
Dreams with lightning.
Dreams with rain
Dreams of dancing pigs!

Esmée Turlej (8)
Yealmpstone Farm Primary School

Dream

Howling wind in my bedroom
Twisting, terrifying is how I felt
Jumping, running like stormy horses
Terrifying in the windy days,
Happy feeling from my mind
The stormy head
Eating chocolate all night long
Feeling tired but calm in my bed.

Tasha Covel (9)
Yealmpstone Farm Primary School

Dreams

Bad dreams,
Good dreams,
Angry dreams,
Which dreams are the best?
Stupid dreams,
Sleepy dreams,
I wonder which dream I will have tonight?

Harrison Nicholls (7)
Yealmpstone Farm Primary School

Magic Horses

Magic horses in the air
Cute fury animals
Under your beds
Horses happily drinking
Chocolate milk from the river.

Sweet air up above and
Nicely shining sun, fluffy clouds
Snowy white horses running
Across the grazing green grass.

Ellie Cartwright (7)
Yealmpstone Farm Primary School

Special Dreams

Dreams are like a made-up massive story
They are exotic fun fast adventures
Like a long-lost adventure that goes on forever
They are a fantastic adventure on a horse that gallops happily
Like a brilliant funny roller coaster that rides dramatically
A giant tall silly wall you have to climb immediately!

Daniel Horton (8)
Yealmpstone Farm Primary School

Dream World

In a land of dreams playful bloodthirsty dinosaurs
Or soft nice quiet bunnies
Nasty horrible dreams
Quiet spooky dreams like the evacuees of World War II
And the deafening sound of the air raid siren.
Lovely homes in your dreams
Up in the nice quiet sky
Having a tea party.
Horrible or nice dreams.
You could ride a big bird or
Car to the nice cold moon.
In your bed you dream of all those things
But never realise that your dreams might be
A door to a world where anything could happen.

Nathan Jones (8)
Yealmpstone Farm Primary School

Young Writers Information

We hope you have enjoyed reading this book - and that you will continue to enjoy it in the coming years.

If you like reading and writing poetry drop us a line, or give us a call, and we'll send you a free information pack.

Alternatively if you would like to order further copies of this book or any of our other titles, then please give us a call or log onto our website at www.youngwriters.co.uk

Young Writers Information
Remus House
Coltsfoot Drive
Peterborough
PE2 9JX
(01733) 890066